The Minehead Branch and the West Somerset Railway

by

Colin G. Maggs

THE OAKWOOD PRESS

British Library Cataloguing in Publication Data
A Record for this book is available from the British Library
ISBN 0 85361 528 4

Typeset by Oakwood Graphics.
Repro by Ford Graphics, Ringwood, Hants.
Printed by Alpha Print (Oxford) Ltd, Witney, Oxford.

'2251' class 0-6-0 No. 2261 of 83B (Taunton) Shed, leaves Minehead on 24th August, 1950.
Revd Alan Newman

Published by
The Oakwood Press
P.O. Box 13, Usk, Mon., NP5 1YS.

Contents

The 4.45 pm Minehead to Taunton leaves Stogumber on 30th June, 1967. It is a Gloucester Railway Carriage & Wagon cross-country dmu with motor second No. W51077 trailing.
Author

'Hymek' diesel-hydraulic No. D7012 with an up train, crosses No. D7079 heading a down train at Williton, June 1967. *Derrick Payne*

Chapter One

Historical Introduction

West Somerset has two important coastal towns: Watchet and Minehead. Watchet, a port for hundreds of years, first saw Viking raiders in AD 918. Trade with South Wales has always been important as the distance is about 130 miles by road and only 16 by sea. During the Civil War, Royalists shipped stores to Watchet from sympathetic South Wales. *Circa* 1682 smuggling salt, wine and brandy was the sole business of several small vessels. A paper mill established *c.* 1750 helped to diversify trade. Watchet has appeared in fiction for it was when on a walk from Nether Stowey to Lynton, Coleridge arrived at Watchet and decided that it would be from Watchet that the Ancient Mariner would set sail on his fateful voyage. The arrival of the railway in 1862 did not discourage shipping, but encouraged it, acting as a feeder or distributor. That year over 500 ships used Watchet arriving with coal and wheat and leaving a few days later with flour, paper, timber and iron ore. An associated industry was shipbuilding and repair. Watchet was a go-ahead town and as early as 1867 was lit by gas and had piped water in 1889. It only became a civil parish in 1901, until then being St Decuman's which embraced Williton as well.

Minehead too has been a port for hundreds of years, Daniel Defoe saying he believed it 'the best port and safest harbour' along the Bristol Channel. In the 17th century Minehead prospered due to its shipping and woollen industry, but declined in the 18th due to the expansion of other ports such as Bristol and Liverpool. At one time, trade with Ireland was particularly important. *Circa* 1800 the economy felt the departure of the abundant herring. As sea trade declined in the 19th century, holidays with romantic scenery and seaside became popular and in the 1880s and 1890s many of the new houses built had apartments to let. Today Minehead is a charming and beautifully situated, relatively quiet seaside resort, a convenient centre for touring Exmoor and the Lorna Doone country. The town itself has three sections: the former fishing village by the quay; the group of cottages by the old church on the hill; and the growing seaside town and holiday camp around the railway station.

Population

St Decuman's		*Watchet*		*Minehead*	
1861	3,196	1901	1,880	1861	1,582
1871	3,244	1911	1,846	1871	1,605
1881	3,233	1921	1,883	1881	1,774
1891	3,127	1931	1,936	1891	2,071
1901	3,302	1951	2,592	1901	2,780
		1961	2,597	1911	3,752
		1971	2,900	1921	6,116
				1931	6,418
				1951	7,486
				1961	7,745
				1971	8,126

ANNO VICESIMO & VICESIMO PRIMO

VICTORIÆ REGINÆ.

Cap. cxlv.

An Act to authorize the Construction of a Railway from *Taunton* to the Harbour of *Watchet*; and for other Purposes relating to the said Railway and Harbour. [17th *August* 1857.]

WHEREAS the making of a Railway from the *Bristol and Exeter* Railway at *Taunton* to *Watchet* in *Somersetshire* would be of public Advantage: And whereas Plans and Sections of the Railway showing the Line and Levels thereof, with Books of Reference to the Plans containing the Names of the Owners or reputed Owners, Lessees or reputed Lessees, and of the Occupiers of the Lands through which the said Railway will pass, have been deposited with the Clerk of the Peace for the said County: And whereas the Persons herein-after named, with others, are willing, at their own Expense, to construct the said Railway: And whereas it is expedient that the said Company should have Power to enter into Arrangements with the Trustees or other Persons for the Time being having the Management or Control of *Watchet* Harbour, and also with the *Bristol and Exeter* Railway Company; but these Objects cannot be accomplished without the Authority of Parliament: May it therefore please Your Majesty that it may be enacted; and be it enacted by the Queen's most Excellent Majesty, by and with the Advice and Consent of the

[*Local.*] 25 *F* Lords

The first page of the Act for constructing a railway from Taunton to Watchet.

Chapter Two

Promoting the West Somerset Railway

The story of the railway to Minehead started on 30th September, 1833 when an unknown person from Carhampton, near Blue Anchor, issued a 'Prospectus for a Rail Road from Minehead on the Bristol Channel, to the English Channel'. This line was to run from Minehead via the Exe Valley, Tiverton and Exeter to the English Channel. The writer said:

> It is known that there is to be a Rail Road from London to Bristol; from the latter place to Minehead by sea is about 45 miles, a distance which in a steam vessel, with the tide, will perform in four hours upon the average; so that London, Bristol, Exeter and all the intermediate places will be brought as much nearer in time, as the difference in time will be which it takes passengers and goods to travel from one place to another on the new line, by steam carriages on the Rail Road and steam packets on the Channel, and that which it now takes to go from the same place to the other same place by common conveyances on ordinary roads.

It is rather curious that the writer did not think that a railway between Bristol and Minehead, or Bristol and Exeter, would be far more convenient than a steam packet.

In 1845 the Somersetshire & North Devon Junction Railway was proposed. With John Hughes as Engineer, it was planned to build a line from the Bristol & Exeter Railway (B&ER) at Bridgwater to Minehead and Ilfracombe, ships sailing from there to Ireland. The same year, a connecting line, the Bristol & English Channels Direct Junction Railway proposed constructing a line from Bridport to Watchet to link with the scheme. However, both plans proved abortive, not even getting as far as an Act of Parliament.

In the 1850s a line between Bridgwater and Watchet was favoured, but the Quantock Hills formed a barrier to a direct line and the cost of tunnelling would have been prohibitive, though such a line was still being suggested as recently as 1923. The alternative, a branch from Norton Fitzwarren two miles west of Taunton, seemed much more feasible.

Influential landowners met at Dunn's Egremont Hotel, Williton, on 9th July, 1856 to provide a railway from their district, and also the West Somerset Mineral Railway (WSMR) then in course of construction from the Somerset Ironworks on the Brendon Hills, to the Bristol & Exeter near Taunton. An additional inducement to build the line was that the Admiralty had sanctioned £10,000 worth of improvements at Watchet Harbour, including a new breakwater giving an area of about 10 acres of harbour where vessels could float at all states of the tide. An advantage of constructing a railway was said to be that boats taking ore to South Wales could return with coal carried cheaply as 'back traffic' which could be distributed from Watchet by rail. The meeting proposed a committee be formed to obtain the best plan from the engineers. The line's estimated cost was £130,000.

A few weeks later, on 27th October, 1856, a meeting was held at the Guildhall, Taunton, for the purpose of promoting the West Somerset Railway (WSR), those attending pledging themselves to support the Directors and Engineer, giving them *carte blanche* to do what they thought fit. The Engineer was none other than Isambard Kingdom Brunel and the WSR was to prove to be one of his final undertakings.

It was anticipated that the WSR would bring an increase in trade with Bridgwater: bricks, general pottery, cement and other products from the alluvial deposits of the River Parrett, the port of Watchet offering the shortest sea route to south-west Wales and avoiding the treacherous and tortuous navigation of the river below Bridgwater. In order to cope with this expected increase in shipping, the above-mentioned harbour improvements were planned.

It was intended that the WSR would make a junction with the West Somerset Mineral Railway, but a difficulty arose over powers for building a line along the pier and this led to the Directors deciding against such a junction, especially as Brunel advised that it would bring the railway to a level unsuitable for any future westward extension. An additional problem was that the WSR was built to the broad gauge, whereas the WSMR had standard gauge.

The WSR Act, 20 & 21 Vict. cap. 66, received Royal Assent on 17th August, 1857. With Sir Peregrine Acland as Chairman, it had powers to construct 14 miles 22 chains of broad gauge line and raise a capital of £120,000, plus loans of £40,000.

The first general meeting of the company was held at Pattison's Castle Hotel, Taunton on 10th February, 1858. James B. Burke had been appointed assistant Engineer and George Furness, the contractor, said that the work could not be carried out for the estimated cost of £90,000 and suggested omitting the Watchet Harbour branch thereby saving £3,500 and keeping costs within that price. He said his contract would be for £86,500, plus £615 for the cost of extra work found necessary when setting out the line. Stations would cost an additional £5,000, but he agreed to accept a third of his payment in shares and charge only £91,000, including stations. Although he proposed starting work on 22nd July, 1858, this date proved premature because insufficient shares had been taken, this causing the Directors to appeal to the district to buy unappropriated capital. An additional problem with which the company had to contend was that some landowners' agents made unreasonable claims so that the total cost of the line threatened to be increased from £120,000 to £150,000.

The B&ER offered to lease the line paying the WSR 55 per cent of the gross receipts, guaranteeing that receipts would not be less than £4,500, thus giving shareholders a return of 3 per cent. The contract with Furness was eventually signed and sealed on 5th April, 1859. On 7th April the first sod was turned at Crowcombe Heathfield and a crowd of several thousand enjoyed the ceremony in fine weather, Sir Peregrine Acland performing the honours at what was to become the Summit Cutting. In addition to the usual polished oak wheelbarrow and spade, a pick axe was also provided. Brunel was absent due to ill health.

The contractor began work at Woolston Moor, south of Williton, on 10th April. George Furness himself looked after the firm's overseas contracts, while those in England, including the WSR, were supervised by Frederick Furness.

Brunel died on 15th September, 1859 and the company Secretary was directed by the Board to convey 'the expression of their deep feeling of sorrow and condolence upon the decease of the late Mr Brunel, and while fully sensible of how much the company have to regret the deprivation of his valuable professional services, they consider the death of one so eminent, a great public loss'. His chief assistant, R.P. Brereton took over the office of Engineer, Burke continuing as assistant.

By 24th September, 1859 work on the summit cutting was well in hand and 15 other cuttings, several bridges and culverts had been started between the 5¾ mile post (east of Crowcombe) and Watchet, this being the heaviest section. In his report on 27th March, 1860 Brereton said that an unusually wet winter had delayed works, but most of the bridges and culverts on the section had been started and near Williton two to three miles of permanent way were to be laid soon. The company intended applying to Parliament for a short extension to Watchet to a better site for the station and more suited for a connection to the quays. The WSR Amendment Act of 15th May, 1860, 23 Vict. cap. 51, authorised this and also the issue of preference shares. Guest & Company's tender for rails was accepted on 14th June, 1860, 1,650 tons being purchased at £6 10*s.* 6*d.* delivered at Watchet for cash, or 5 per cent preference shares at a discount.

On 25th September, 1860 Brereton reported that works from Doniford to Combe Florey were either finished, or in a very forward state. Some ballasting had taken place near Williton and the permanent way was soon to be laid, 300 tons of rail having been delivered, though on 14th February, 1861 he said that the weather had been unfavourable for ballasting, and laying the permanent way had yet to be commenced. In the spring and summer matters improved and on 6th August, 1861 Furness anticipated that the line could be opened to Williton in early October. Things did not appear to be quite so rosy on 7th September, 1861 when the half-yearly meeting was told that earthworks were complete, except for cuttings at Watchet and the summit near Crowcombe Heathfield, a few bridges were still incomplete and 8½ miles of permanent way had been laid, most of the 1,600 tons of rail having being delivered. Construction of the stations was in progress and it was anticipated that the line would be completed by the end of November. From these facts, the Directors deemed it advisable not to open the WSR until the whole line was ready. On 14th November, 1861 Frederick Furness said he was disappointed not to have had an engine for the ballasting, but nevertheless the line would be ready by 24th December for the Board of Trade Inspector. Three days later the WSR minutes stated: 'Much dissatisfaction was expressed by the Board at there being no likelihood of the Railway being ready for opening by the time promised by Mr Furness'. On 16th January, 1862 Brereton was 'not satisfied with the progress of the works', but Frederick Furness assured the Directors that the line would be ready by 16th February, though events proved this promise to be false.

The contractors experienced problems with petty theft on 5th January, 1862 when Mark Langdon stole an 'iron chair from a signal' at Newton Cutting, north of Stogumber station. The stolen item was the property of Messrs Hennet, Spink & Else, ironfounders of Bridgwater who held the signalling contract.

By 8th February Williton and Stogumber stations had been completed and Bishop's Lydeard and Crowcombe required little more than painting. Watchet was roofed in, but the engine shed remained incomplete. Signals had been erected and the mile posts were being fixed. The line was to be ready by 10th March. The 1861 census revealed that the WSR contract had 221 men with 232 women and children as dependants, but at the peak period, 334 men and 34 horses had been employed.

On 6th March, 1862 a Bristol & Exeter locomotive and 'truck' (perhaps a brake van), left Norton Junction and ran non-stop to Williton where it was welcomed by the Chairman Sir Peregrine Acland. It proceeded to Watchet arriving about 3.00 pm. There the engine was turned, the points tested, water taken on and it returned to Taunton. On 31st March Brereton reported that the work of building goods sheds would start at once.

Captain F.H. Rich carried out the Board of Trade inspection on 8th March, 1862. His train hauled by B&ER 4-4-0ST No. 51 left Taunton at 9.00 am, arrived at Williton at 3.00 pm where he lunched at the Egremont Hotel before continuing to Watchet. He did not pass the line because, perhaps due to haste, the lodges at each of the two level crossings were of timber, whereas Rich insisted they be constructed in brick. He therefore made a second inspection on 15th March when he reported:

To the Secretary
Railway Dept
Board of Trade

Board of Trade
17th March, 1862

Sir,

I have the honor [*sic*] to report for the information of the Lords of the Committee of Privy Council for Trade, that, in accordance with your minute of the 5th Inst., I inspected the West Somerset Railway, which extends from the 165th mile post from London, on the Bristol & Exeter Railway, near Taunton, to the town of Watchet, on the West Coast of England.

I had previously inspected this Railway, on the 7th [in fact 8th, *author*] Inst., but could not report it complete in consequence of there being no lodges at the level crossings and several minor points unfinished.

The length of the line is 14 m. 54 ch. It is single throughout with sidings at each station, *vide*: Bishop's Lydeard, Heathfield Crowcombe, Stogumber, Williton and Watchet.

The width of the line at formation level is 17 feet in cuttings and 21 feet on embankments. The guage [*sic*] is 7 ft 0¼ in. The intervals between the lines of rails, where they are double, are 6 feet.

The bridge rail, in lengths of 18 feet and 20 feet, weighing 62 lbs per lineal yard, is fixed to longitudinal sleepers 12 in. by 6 in. with transoms 4½ in. by 6 in.

The switches are of the ordinary pattern in use on the broad gauge.

The ballast is in some cases gravel, in others broken stone and shingle. Its average depth is 1 ft 6 in.

There are eleven over bridges of various spaces, from 15 ft to 46 ft 6 in. One of these has cast-iron girders, the rest are constructed of masonry and brick.

Seventeen under bridges of spans varying from 14 ft 4 in. to 50 feet. Four of these have wrought iron girders, the rest are built of stone, brick and mortar. The whole of the bridges are well and substantially constructed.

There are two public level crossings - one at 7 m. 55 ch. and the other at 8 m. 36 ch. The gates close across the road and railway. Distant signals as well as discs [and] 2 lamps on the gates, are provided. The lodges for the gate keepers, which were not commenced when I inspected the line on the 7th, [are] all now built of brick to a height of about 7 ft and will be completed before the end of the month.

There are wooden sentry boxes for intermediate use. A brick lodge is also building at the Junction with the Bristol and Exeter Railway near Taunton, for the signalman. Indicators are attached to all facing points. An engine turntable is provided at Watchet and another at Taunton.

The line is to be worked by the Bristol and Exeter Railway Co. The undertaking as to the proposed mode of working which I enclose, is signed by the Chairman and Secretary of both companies, and appears satisfactory.

I beg, therefore, to report that the West Somerset Railway from near Taunton to Watchet, may be opened for passenger traffic.

I have the honor
to be sir
Yr obedient servant
F.H. Rich
Capt Royl Engrs

The line was formally opened on 27th March, 1862, the *West Somerset Free Press* recording:

At about 3 o'clock in the afternoon three carriages attached to an engine arrived at Watchet, bringing several of the Directors as well as those connected with the Bristol and Exeter line . . . At the entrance to the station a triumphal arch was erected, and amidst a bevy of evergreens and flags we noticed a motto: 'Welcome ye Friends of Progress'. A celebratory dinner was held in a room above the Market House, Watchet. Williton was also decorated with flags, banners and a triumphal arch, while a more unusual feature was decorated fir trees planted on either side of streets.

The WSR was opened to the public on 31st March, 1862. That day a special was worked from Taunton to provide a locomotive and stock to work the first up train. The first down train, the 10.35 am from Taunton was crowded, while 'the next train was so full that occupants were obliged to form rows two deep in each carriage'. At Williton crowds were immense for the 2.49 pm train from Watchet and 'each one seemed afraid they would not get a ticket and one passenger even offered 2*d*. or 3*d*. more to be served first'.

The opening date of the branch was most convenient for the Bristol & Exeter because from 3rd February, 1863 the Somerset Central Railway had ceased to be worked by the B&ER, and so stock hitherto used on the SCR was transferred to WSR. As the goods sheds were not ready, freight traffic did not commence until August.

On 8th May, 1862 Furness signed an additional contract to complete Watchet station and goods shed and lay more track, the total paid to him being £105,020 13*s*. 9*d*. In the half-yearly report given on 30th September, 1862 it was stated that goods sheds at Bishop's Lydeard, Stogumber, Williton and Watchet were complete together with the sidings at Watchet Harbour. The average receipts

View of Watchet soon after opening. Contractors' wagons stand on the harbour sidings, right foreground. Centre left is the timber-built engine shed with the goods shed in the distance.
Courtesy: H.H. Hole

for the previous 12 weeks had been £150 per week and a large increase was anticipated when the goods traffic was fully developed. That month the B&ER asked that the goods sheds 'be enclosed' (doors fitted?), offering to carry out the work for £247.

At the half-yearly meeting on 28th March, 1863 it was announced that the line was complete except for a lime loading dock at Watchet. Traffic for the first 51 weeks totalled £5,893, averaging a little under £8 per mile per week. Expenditure to December on the line had been £166,612 and its total cost eventually reached £180,634 13*s*. 8*d*. - rather more than Brunel's 1856 estimate of £130,000. A year later when the Minehead Railway was proposed, in view of the WSR's financial position, the WSR Directors did not feel justified in recommending the company to subscribe towards it. Furness' liability to maintain the WSR expired on 31st March, 1863, this responsibility being taken over by the working company, the Bristol & Exeter.

The WSR was not entirely satisfied with the way the B&ER worked the line. In September 1867 the WSR Secretary wrote complaining that trucks were not available for conveying goods, and the promised weighbridge had yet to be installed. Then in May 1868 coal and coke charges were questioned. The maximum authorised by the WSR Act was 2*d*. per ton per mile, yet the B&ER charged:

	Miles	*Amount charged*	*Amount authorised by WSR Act*
Watchet-Taunton	17	51*d*.	34*d*.
Watchet-Bishop's Lydeard	12	36*d*.	24*d*.
Watchet-Crowcombe	8	36*d*.	16*d*.
Watchet-Stogumber	6	36*d*.	12*d*.
Watchet-Williton	2	36*d*.	6*d*.

The WSR observed that the lines to Watchet Harbour were constructed to be worked by locomotives, yet a special charge of 2*d*. over the mileage rates quoted above was made to traders using these lines, even though the merchants themselves loaded and unloaded coal and themselves hauled the trucks from the harbour to the station. The B&ER's reply was long delayed. Despite further correspondence on the subject, the B&ER was still overcharging and a 'considerable trade at Watchet is being diverted in consequence'. On 6th November, 1868 the WSR stated:

	Amount authorised		*Terminal fee*	*Total*		*Amount charged by B&ER*		*Excess charge*
	s.	*d.*	*d.*	*s.*	*d.*	*s.*	*d.*	*d.*
Watchet-Taunton	2	1½	6	2	7½	3	4½	9
Watchet-Bishop's Lydeard	2	0	6	2	6	2	8	2
Watchet-Crowcombe	1	4	6	1	10	2	0	2
Watchet-Stogumber	1	0	6	1	6	1	8	2
Watchet-Williton		6	6	1	0	1	2	2

Miles	PASSENGER TRAINS. UP.	ON WEEK DAYS.																						SUNDAYS.		
		1 2	1 2	X F 1 2 3	X 1 2	X 1 2	X 1 2	X G 1 2	1 2	Exp 1 2	X 1 2	X H 1 2	1 2	X 1 2	1 2	L X 1 2	K Mail 1 2	X 1 2	X 1 2	X 1 2	X 1 2	1 2	Mail 1 2	X 1 2 3	Mail 1 2	Mail 1 2
		a.m	a.m	a.m	a.m	a.m	a.m	a.m	p.m	a.m	p.m	a.m	a.m	p.m	p.m.	p.m	p.m	p.m	p.m	p.m	p.m	p.m	p.m	a.m	p.m	p.m
	Plymouth .. dep							6 35		8 35		9 5	10 25			12 35	2 15				4 10	6 0	7 45	6 40	12 40	7 45
	Exeter .. arr.							9 25		10 25		11 40	12 20			3 15	4 35				6 50	8 50	10 2	9 28	3 15	10 2
	EXETER .. dep			6 0	8 0	8 50		9 45		10 30		11 45	12 25			3 30	4 45			6 0	7 30	9 5	10 12	9 40	3 30	10 12
3½	Stoke Canon ..			6 11	8 9	8 59						11 55								6 11	7 38	9 14		9 51		
7½	Silverton ..			6 22	8 18	9 8														6 22	7 46	9 23		10 2		
8¾	Hele and Bradninch ..			6 28	8 25	9 15						12 7				3 48				6 28	7 52	9 30		10 8	3 45	
12¾	Cullompton ..			6 40	8 34	9 21						12 18				3 59				6 40	8 0	9 39		10 20	3 55	
14¾	Tiverton Junction ..			6 48	8 42	9 32		10 15				12 27	S			4 7	S			6 49	8 7	9 47		10 29	4 2	
19¾	Tiverton .. dep					9 18		10 0				12 12				3 49				6 30	7 52			10 14	3 46	
	Tiverton .. arr				8 57			10 30				1 4	1 4			4 22	5 23			7 4	8 20	10 10		10 44	4 18	
19¾	Burlescombe ..			7 1		9 41														7 3	8 19			10 43		
23¾	Wellington ..			7 14		9 52		10 35				12 45				4 23				7 17	8 31			10 57	4 13	
28¾	Norton Fitzwarren ..			7 28		10 0		10 46				12 55	1 8			4 35				7 33	8 40			11 13	4 29	
	Chard Branch																									
	Chard .. dep			6 0				9 40		9 40		12 20	12 20			3 45				6 50						
4	Ilminster ..			6 26				9 50		9 50		12 30	12 30			3 55				7 0						
8¾	Hatch ..			6 56				10 4		10 4		12 44	12 44			4 9				7 14						
12½	Thorne ..			7 10				10 15		10 15		12 55	12 55			4 20				7 25						
15¼	Taunton .. arr			7 20				10 25		10 25		1 5	1 5			4 30				7 35						
	W. Somset. Branch.																									
	Minehead .. dep																									
1½	Dunster ..																									
3½	Blue Anchor ..																									
5¾	Washford ..																									
8	Watchet ..			6 0				9 45		9 45		12 0	12 0			3 35				6 35	9 0					
9½	Williton ..			6 10				9 51		9 51		12 6	12 6			3 41				6 41	9 6					
13	Stogumber ..			6 23				10 2		10 2		12 19	12 19			3 53				6 54	9 15					
15¼	Crowcombe Heathfield			6 35				10 10		10 10		12 26	12 26			4 1				7 0	9 23					
19½	Bishop's Lydeard ..			6 57		T		10 18		10 18		12 31	12 34			4 9				7 9	9 31					
22¼	Norton Fitzwarren ..			7 15		1 2 3		10 28		10 28		12 45	12 45			4 20				7 20	9 40					
24½	Taunton .. arr			7 20		Class		10 33		10 33		12 50	12 50			4 25				7 25	9 45					
	Devon and Somerset Branch.																									
	Barnstaple .. dep.					7 10		9 15		9 15		10 30	10 30			2 0	3 30			5 25	9 0					
3¾	Swimbridge ..					7 53						10 43	10 43			2 13				5 35	9 10					
7	Castle Hill ..					8 5						10 55	10 55			2 25				5 44	9 19					
10¼	South Molton ..					8 18		9 47		9 47		11 8	11 8			2 38	3 57			5 56	9 31					
14½	Bps. Nympton & Molland					8 33						11 23	11 23			2 53				6 9						
19¾	East Anstey ..					8 49						11 39	11 39			3 9				6 22						
23¼	Dulverton ..					9 6		10 14		10 14		11 51	11 51			3 21	4 27			6 36						
26½	Morebath (for Bampton)					9 11						12 1	12 1			3 31				6 45						
30½	Venn Cross ..					9 21						12 12	12 12			3 42				6 55						
35¼	Wiveliscombe ..					9 37		10 38		10 38		12 26	12 26			3 58	4 53			7 8						
38	Milverton ..					9 45						12 36	12 36			4 8				7 16						
42¼	Norton Fitzwarren ..					9 58		10 52		10 52		12 49	12 49			4 22	5 9			7 29						
44½	Taunton .. arr.					10 5		10 58		10 58		12 55	12 55			4 32	5 15			7 35						
30¾	Taunton .. arr							10 51				1 0									8 45					
	Taunton .. dep			7 36		10 10		11 15		11 9		1 20	1 15			4 42	5 31			7 40			11 12	11 20	4 36	11 12
	W.S.&W.																									
	Weymouth .. dep			5 30									9 29			12 30				5 10						
	Yeovil .. arr			6 20									10 40			1 30				6 10						
	Yeovil Branch																									
	Yeovil .. dep			6 30	N. Guage			10 30					12 0	N. Guage		3 45	N. Guage			6 35	N. Guage					
7	Martock ..			6 45				10 45					12 12			3 59				6 50						
12	Langport ..			6 57				10 57					12 23			4 12				7 2						
16½	Athelney ..			7 8				11 8					12 34			4 25				7 13						
19	Durston ..			7 20				11 20					1 5			4 45				7 25						
25	Taunton ..							11 35																		
25	Bridgwater .. arr		N. G.										1 20													
36¾	Durston ..		8 0	7 52		10 23		11 31				1 36				4 55				7 56				11 35	4 49	
42½	Bridgwater ..		8 25	8 9		10 37		11 47				1 52	1 37			5 9	5 51			8 13			11 37	11 54	5 2	11 37
44½	Dunball ..		8 33	8 17								2 0								8 21						
	Som. & Dor. Rail.																									
	Poole (Town) .. dep							8 10				10 45	10 45			1 30										
	Wells ..			7 35			10 35	10 35				12 45	12 45			4 35				6 20						
	Glastonbury ..			7 50			10 50	11 25				1 0	1 0			4 55				6 35						
	Highbridge .. arr			8 25			11 20	11 55				1 22	1 22			5 19				7 7						
	Burnham .. dep			8 15								1 20	1 20			4 0				8 15						
48¾	Highbridge ..		8 48	8 32	1 2	10 50		12 3				2 15	1 50			5 23				8 33				12 12	5 15	
55	Bleadon and Uphill			8 48	Class							2 31				5 39				8 48						
57	Weston-s.-Mare Junction ..	6 55	8 45	9 0	10 5	11 5		12 26			12 47	2 40	2 5		4 0	5 46			7 36	8 56		9 50		12 39	5 30	
58½	Weston-s.-Mare dep	6 50	8 40	8 50	10 0	10 55		12 11			12 40	2 30	1 55		3 55	5 30			7 30	8 30		9 45		12 29	5 20	
	Weston-s.-Mare arr			9 29		11 20		12 40				2 55	2 20			6 0				9 10				12 49	5 40	
60	Worle ..	7 3		9 9							12 56	2 49			4 8				7 42	9 3				12 48		
	Cheddar Valley Branch.																									
	Wells .. dep	5 45	7 45	7 45			9 40				11 53			2 20				5 30		7 50						
1	Wookey ..	5 50	7 50	7 50			9 45				11 59							5 35								
3½	Lodge Hill ..	5 59	7 59	7 59			9 54				12 8			2 29				5 44		7 59						
5¾	Draycott ..	6 6	8 6	8 6			10 1				12 16			2 36				5 51		8 7						
8	Cheddar ..	6 13	8 13	8 13			10 8				12 24			2 44				5 58		8 15						
9½	Axbridge ..	6 20	8 20	8 20			10 15				12 30			2 50				6 5		8 21						
12	Winscombe ..	6 27	8 27	8 27			10 22				12 37			2 59				6 12		8 30						
13	Sandford and Banwell ..	6 32	8 32	8 32			10 27				12 42			3 5				6 17		8 36						
16	Congresbury ..	6 40	8 40	8 40			10 35							3 14				6 25		8 45						
17½	Yatton .. arr	6 45	8 45	8 45			10 40				12 51			3 18				6 30		8 50						
63½	Yatton ..	7 11	8 56	9 22	10 17	11 15	10 42		12 22		1 5	3 2		3 20	4 17	6 1		6 50	7 50	9 15		9 59		12 56	5 45	
67½	Clevedon .. dep	7 0	8 40	9 10	10 3	10 41			12 10		12 10	2 47			4 5	5 49		6 20	7 38	8 53		9 45		12 44	5 30	
	Clevedon .. arr	7 23	9 8	9 34	10 29	11 50	11 7				2 11	3 14		3 55	4 32	6 13		6 50	8 2	9 27		10 11		1 8	5 57	
67¼	Nailsea ..	7 20	9 6	9 30					12 32		1 15	3 10			4 27	6 12		6 59		9 22				1 5	5 56	
70	Bourton ..	7 26	9 13	9 38							1 23	3 18			4 33			7 5		9 29						
	Bedminster ..	7 40	9 27	9 57	10 37	11 37	11 2	1 2	12 47		1 37	3 37	2 32	3 41	4 47	6 27	6 42	7 20	8 12	9 47				1 27	6 12	
75	**BRISTOL** .. arr	7 43	9 30	10 0	10 40	11 40	11 5	1 5	12 50	12 4	1 40	3 49	2 35	3 43	4 50	6 30	6 45	7 23	8 15	9 50		10 25	12 32	1 30	6 15	12 32
	Bristol .. dep	7 50	10 10	10 10		12 9		1 15	1 15	12 9	2 45	3 50	2 45	3 50		7 0	7 0						12 50	1 45	6 30	12 50
193	Paddington .. arr.	10 45	2 30	2 30		2 45		5 15	5 15	2 45	6 0	9 10	6 0	9 10		10 20	10 20						4 35	7 15	11 10	4 35

(First 1 2 column) On Mondays a Train will leave Weston at 6.50 a.m., Weston Junc. 6.55, Yatton 7.7, Clevedon 6.55, Nailsea 7.16, Bedminster 7.32, arriving at Bristol at 7.35. — On Thursdays only.

S Slip Car detached at Tiverton Junc. for Tiverton at 12.49 p.m.

S Slip Carriage detached at Tiverton Junc. for Tiverton at 5.9 p.m.

On Mondays, Wednesdays and Saturdays only.

On Mondays and Thursdays only.

F Third Class to all Local Stations, and to Stations on the Great Western at which the Train stops, except from Exeter to Paddington: and also to Gloucester, Cheltenham, Worcester, and Birmingham, from Exeter, Taunton, Yeovil, Bridgwater, Weston and Clevedon, by the Midland Railway Co.'s Train leaving Bristol at 1.15 p.m.; and to certain Stations north of Birmingham, proceeding from Bristol at 10.15 a.m. Van Parcels conveyed by this Train. Third Class from Yeovil Branch to all Up and Down Stations. G Third Class from Exeter to all Local Stations at which the Train stops, and to all Great Western Stations at which the Train stops. Third Class from South Devon Stations, St. Thomas inclusive, to Bristol and Exeter and Great Western Stations; also Third Class Tiverton, Barnstaple and South Molton to Paddington and Reading. H Third Class from Kingsbridge Road and Tiverton to all Local Stations, and Stations on the Great Western, at which the Train stops. Meat Vans conveyed by this Train. K Third Class from Falmouth, Penzance, and intermediate Stations to St German's inclusive, to Bristol and Exeter and Great Western Stations; also from Saltash, Devonport and South Devon Stations to Paddington. Third Class from Falmouth and Truro to Birmingham. Third Class from Exeter and from Barnstaple and South Molton to Paddington. L Third Class Exeter to Waterford. X Horses and Carriages conveyed by these Trains. The Bedminster Station will be used as an arrival Station only on the Up Line. T Third Class from Devon and Somerset Stations to all Local Stations and to certain Stations on Great Western and Midland Railways.

For the convenience of Passengers attending the Tiverton Market on TUESDAYS, a Train will run from the Junction to Tiverton on arrival of the 6 0 a.m. Train from Exeter.

Working timetable for August 1874 for up passenger trains.

Miles	PASSENGER TRAINS. DOWN.	Mail 1 2	Mail 1 2	X 1 2	X 1 2	X B 1 2 3	X 1 2	C X 1 2	1 2	X 1 2	X 1 2	D 1 2	X 1 2	1 2	Exp 1 2	X E 1 2	X 1 2	1 2	1 2	X M 1 2	1 2	X 1 2	SUNDAYS. Mail 1 2	SUNDAYS. 1 2 3	SUNDAYS. X 1 2
	Paddington .. .. ..dep	8 10	..	..	..	..	..	6 45	..	..	..	9 0	..	..	11 45	10 30	..	..	..	1 50	5 0	5 0	8 10	..	10 0
	Bristol .. .. arr.	12 5	..	..		..	..	10 15	..	..	..	12 15	..	..	2 21	3 5	..	..	..	5 50	8 5	8 5	12 5	..	3 3[illegible]
		a.m	a.m	a.m	a.m	a.m	a.m	a.m	a.m	a.m	p.m	p.m	p.m	p.m	p.m	p.m	p.m	p.m	p.m	p.m	p.m	p.m	a.m	a.m	p.m
	BRISTOL .. .. .. dep	12 30	6 15	7 25	..	8 10	9 50	10 30	11 10	11 30	12 10	12 30	1 30	2 0	2 26	3 15	4 0	4 40	5 15	6 0	8 15	8 35	12 30	6 30	3 40
	Bedminster	..	..	..	..	8 15	..	..	11 15	..	..	..	..	..	..	..	..	4 45	..	..	..	8 40	..	..	..
5½	Bourton	..	..	..	..	8 29	10 0	..	..	..	..	..	1 39	..	..	..	..	4 57	..	6 14	..	8 48	..	..	..
8	Nailsea	..	..	7 39	..	8 39	10 5	..	11 28	..	..	..	1 48	..	..	*	..	5 6	..	6 22	..	8 55	..	6 48	3 5[illegible]
12	Yatton	..	..	7 49	..	8 52	10 15	10 55	11 38	11 53	12 35	12 52	1 59	..	..	3 42	4 20	5 17	Y	6 34	..	9 5	..	6 59	4 [illegible]
16	Clevedon.. .. dep	..	..	7 37	..	8 40	10 3	10 41	11 26	11 26	12 10	12 10	..	..	..	3 28	4 5	..	..	6 20	..	8 53	..	6 47	3 5[illegible]
	Clevedon.. .. arr	..	..	8 1	..	9 8	10 29	11 7	11 50	..	..	..	2 11	..	..	3 55	4 32	5 29	5 47	6 50	..	9 27	..	7 10	4 2[illegible]
	Cheddar Valley Branch.																								
	Yatton .. .. .. dep	..	..	..	..	9 30	..	..	..	11 55	..	1 10	..	..	..	..	4 23	..	..	6 45	..	9 18	..	..	..
1½	Congresbury	..	..	..	..	9 35	..	..	..	12 0	..	1 15	..	..	..	..	4 28	..	..	6 50	..	9 23	..	..	..
4½	Sandford and Banwell..	..	..	..	..	9 44	..	..	..	12 7	..	1 23	..	..	..	..	4 36	..	..	6 58	..	9 31	..	..	..
5½	Winscombe	..	..	..	..	9 49	..	..	..	12 12	..	1 28	..	..	..	..	4 41	..	..	7 3	..	9 36	..	..	..
8	Axbridge	..	..	..	..	9 58	..	..	..	12 18	..	1 35	..	..	..	..	4 48	..	..	7 10	..	9 43	..	..	..
9½	Cheddar	..	..	..	..	10 11	..	..	..	12 24	..	1 42	..	..	..	..	4 55	..	..	7 17	..	9 50	..	..	..
11¾	Draycott	..	..	..	..	10 19	..	..	..	12 32	..	1 49	..	..	..	..	5 2	..	..	7 24	..	9 57	..	..	..
14	Lodge Hill	..	..	..	..	10 27	..	..	..	12 40	..	1 56	..	..	..	..	5 9	..	..	7 31	..	10 4	..	..	..
16½	Wookey	..	..	..	..	10 36	..	..	..	12 49	..	2 5	..	..	..	..	5 18	..	..	7 40	..	10 13	..	..	..
17½	Wells .. .. .. arr	..	..	..	..	10 42	..	..	..	12 55	..	2 10	..	..	..	..	5 23	..	..	7 45	..	10 18	..	..	..
15½	Worle	..	..	7 57	..	9 4	10 23	..	11 45	..	12 44	..	..	2 28	..	..	..	..	5 43	..	..	9 13	..	7 8	4 1[illegible]
18½	Weston-s.-Mare Junction ..	..	6 43	8 7	..	9 14	10 35	11 5	11 53	..	12 53	1 7	..	2 35	..	4 1	..	..	5 50	6 50	8 41	9 23	..	7 17	4 2[illegible]
20	Weston-s.-Mare dep	..	6 33	..	..	8 50	..	10 55	..	..	12 40	12 55	..	..	..	3 46	..	..	..	6 40	8 30	..	..	7 7	4 1[illegible]
	Weston-s.-Mare arr	..	6 58	8 15	..	9 29	10 40	11 20	12 0	..	1 22	1 22	..	2 40	..	4 15	..	..	5 55	7 5	9 10	9 30	..	7 27	4 3[illegible]
20½	Bleadon and Uphill	..	..	..	N. G.	9 24	..	11 13	..	..	..	..	..	..	..	4 9	..	..	..	6 56	..	..	..	..	..
27	Highbridge	..	6 58	..	9 15	9 42	..	11 29	..	..	1 10	1 26	..	..	..	4 27	..	..	..	7 11	8 56	..	..	7 31	4 44
	Som. & Dor. Rail.																								
	Burnham .. .. .. arr	..	8 10	..	..	..	..	12 15	..	..	..	2 0	..	..	..	5 35	..	..	..	7 25	9 35	..	..	..	..
	Highbridge .. .. dep	..	7 10	8 38	9 6	..	..	12 26	..	..	..	1 35	2 5	..	..	4 32	..	..	..	9 7		..	..	..	..
	Glastonbury .. .. arr	..	7 45	9 0	9 34	..	..	12 58	..	..	..	1 57	2 40	..	..	5 0	..	..	..	9 35	..	..	..	..	..
	Wells..	..	8 30	9 50	9 50	..	..	1 15	..	..	..	3 0	3 0	..	..	5 20	..	..	..	9 50	..	..	..	..	..
	Poole (Town)..	..	11 50	11 50		..	..		..	..	..	4 10		..	..	9 25	..	..	..		..	..	..	..	..
30¾	Dunball	..	..	..	9 35	9 56	..	..	..	..	1 21	..	..	..	..	4 37	..	..	..	7 22	..	..	..	..	..
33	Bridgwater	1 23	7 11	..	9 40	10 4	..	11 44	..	..	1 29	1 38	..	..	S	4 45	..	..	..	7 31	9 9	..	1 23	7 49	4 5[illegible]
39	Durston	..	7 24	..		10 21	..	11 59	..	..	..	..	..	..	..	5 0	..	..	..	7 47	..	..	..	8 3	5 1[illegible]
	Yeovil Branch					N. G.						N. G.				N. G.				N. G.					
	Bridgwater .. .. dep	..	..	..	..	..	..	..	..	..	..	1 45	..	..	..	..	..	..	..	..	..	..	..	..	..
	Taunton	..	..	..	..	..	..	11 45	..	..	..	..	..	..	..	..	..	..	..	..	..	..	..	..	..
	Durston	..	8 5	..	..	10 30	..	12 0	..	..	..	2 10	..	..	..	5 10	..	..	..	8 0	..	..	..	..	..
2½	Athelney	..	8 10	..	..	10 35	..	12 5	..	..	..	2 15	..	..	..	5 16	..	..	..	8 6	..	..	..	..	..
7	Langport	..	8 26	..	..	10 58	..	12 24	..	..	..	2 35	..	..	..	5 30	..	..	..	8 20	..	..	..	..	..
12	Martock	..	8 42	..	..	11 15	..	12 39	..	..	..	2 52	..	..	..	5 40	..	..	..	8 30	..	..	..	..	..
19	Yeovil .. .. .. arr	..	9 0	..	..	11 35	..	12 54	..	..	..	3 10	..	..	..	6 2	..	..	..	8 52	..	..	..	..	..
	W. S. W. Yeovil .. .. .. dep	..	9 25	..	..	12 22	..	2 40	..	..	..	5 5	..	..	..	..	..	..	..	9 40	..	..	..	..	..
	Weymouth .. .. arr	..	10 40	1 & 2	..	1 40	..	3 45	..	..	..	6 25	..	..	..	..	..	..	..	10 35	..	..	..	..	..
44¾	Taunton .. .. .. arr	..	..	..	..	10 38	..	..	..	..	1 55	..	..	..	..	..	..	..	..	..	..	..	..	..	..
	Taunton .. .. .. dep	1 48	7 37	7 0	..	10 43	..	12 14	..	..		2 8	..	3 23	3 18	5 19	..	..	..	8 5	9 33	..	1 48	8 18	5 2[illegible]
	Devon and Somerset Branch.																								
	Taunton .. .. .. dep	..	7 50	..	..	10 45	..	1 0	..	..	..	..	..	..	3 30	5 35	..	..	..	8 15	..	..	..	..	..
2	Norton Fitzwarren ..	..	7 59	..	..	10 52	..	1 6	..	..	..	..	..	..	3 36	5 41	..	..	..	8 24	..	..	..	..	..
6½	Milverton	..	8 14	..	..	11 5	..	1 17	..	..	..	..	..	..	3 47	5 52	..	..	..	8 39	..	..	..	..	..
9½	Wiveliscombe	..	8 26	..	..	11 15	..	1 28	..	..	..	..	..	..	3 58	6 3	..	..	..	8 51	..	..	..	..	..
14	Venn Cross	..	8 41	..	..	11 29	..	1 42	..	..	..	..	..	..	..	6 17	..	..	..	9 6	..	..	..	..	..
17½	Morebath (for Bampton)	..	8 54	..	..	11 40	..	1 51	..	..	..	..	..	..	..	6 26	..	..	..	9 19	..	..	..	..	..
21	Dulverton	..	9 6	..	..	11 51	..	2 2	..	..	..	..	..	..	4 27	6 36	..	..	..	9 31	..	..	..	..	..
24¾	East Anstey	..	9 20	..	..	12 5	..	2 14	..	..	..	..	..	..	..	6 48	..	..	..	9 45	..	..	..	..	..
29¾	Bps. Nympton & Molland	..	9 34	..	..	12 19	..	2 26	..	..	..	..	..	..	..	7 0	..	..	..	9 59	..	..	..	..	..
34½	South Molton..	..	9 47	..	..	12 32	..	2 38	..	..	..	..	..	..	4 55	7 15	..	..	..	10 12	..	..	..	..	..
37½	Castle Hill	..	9 57	..	..	12 42	..	2 48	..	..	..	..	..	..	..	7 23	..	..	..	10 22	..	..	..	..	..
40½	Swimbridge	..	10 7	..	..	12 52	..	2 58	..	..	..	..	..	..	..	7 33	..	..	..	10 32	..	..	..	..	..
44½	Barnstaple .. .. arr	..	10 20	..	..	1 5	..	3 10	..	..	..	..	..	..	5 15	7 45	..	..	..	10 45	..	..	..	..	..
	W. Somset. Branch.																					On Mondays and Thursdays only			
	Taunton .. .. .. dep	..	8 0	..	..	10 58	..	..	..	..	2 10	2 10	..	..	..	5 30	..	..	..	8 10	9 55		..	..	..
2	Norton Fitzwarren ..	..	8 5	..	..	11 3	..	..	..	..	2 15	2 15	..	..	..	5 35	..	..	..	8 15	10 0		..	..	..
5	Bishop's Lydeard	..	8 15	..	..	11 10	..	..	..	..	2 21	2 21	..	..	..	5 46	..	..	..	8 21	10 9		..	..	..
9	Crowcombe Heathfield	..	8 32	..	..	11 24	..	..	..	..	2 35	2 35	..	..	..	5 58	..	..	..	8 35	10 23		..	..	..
11½	Stogumber	..	8 41	..	..	11 31	..	..	..	..	2 42	2 42	..	..	..	6 4	..	..	..	8 42	10 30		..	..	..
15	Williton	..	8 52	..	..	11 40	..	..	..	..	2 51	2 51	..	..	..	6 12	..	..	..	8 51	10 39		..	..	..
16½	Watchet	..	9 0	..	..	11 46	..	..	..	..	2 57	2 57	..	..	..	6 18	..	..	..	8 57	10 45		..	..	..
18¾	Washford..	..	..	..	..	..	..	..	..	..	..	..	..	..	..	..	..	..	..	..	..	..	..	..	..
21	Blue Anchor	..	..	..	..	..	..	..	..	..	..	..	..	..	..	..	..	..	..	..	..	..	..	..	..
23	Dunster	..	..	..	..	..	..	..	..	..	..	..	..	..	..	..	..	..	..	..	..	..	..	..	..
24¾	Minehead.. .. .. arr	..	..	..	..	..	..	..	..	..	..	..	..	..	..	..	..	..	..	..	..	..	..	..	..
	Chard Branch																					On Mondays, Wednesdays and Saturdays only			
	Taunton .. .. .. dep	..	8 0	..	..	11 0	..	..	..	..	2 10	2 10	..	..	..	5 34	..	..	..	8 10	..		..	..	..
3	Thorne	..	8 10	..	..	11 10	..	..	..	..	2 20	2 20	..	..	..	5 44	..	..	..	8 20	..		..	..	..
6½	Hatch	..	8 25	..	..	11 25	..	..	..	..	2 35	2 35	..	..	..	5 59	..	..	..	8 35	..		..	..	..
11½	Ilminster..	..	8 41	..	..	11 41	..	..	..	..	2 51	2 51	..	..	..	6 15	..	..	..	8 51	..		..	..	..
15½	Chard .. .. .. arr	..	8 55	..	..	11 55	..	..	..	..	3 5	3 5	..	..	..	6 29	..	..	..	9 5	..		..	..	..
46¾	Norton Fitzwarren	..	..	7 5	..	10 50	..	..	..	..	..	..	..	3 20	..	5 25	..	..	..	8 12	..		..	..	..
51¾	Wellington	..	..	7 19	..	11 6	..	12 30	..	..	..	..	..	3 42	..	5 40	..	..	..	8 26	..		..	8 31	5 44
56½	Burlescombe	..	..	7 29	..	11 23	..	..	..	..	..	..	..	3 54	..	..	..	..	..	8 40	..		..	..	5 57
60¾	Tiverton Junction	..	8 5	7 39	9 35	11 35	..	12 50	..	..	..	2 42	..	4 6	..	6 2	..	..	..	8 50	9 57	10 30	..	8 54	6 8
65¾	Tiverton .. .. dep	..	7 50	..	9 18	11 15	..	12 12	..	..	..	2 25	..	3 49	..	5 47	..	..	..	8 35	9 40	10 15	..	8 39	5 55
	Tiverton .. .. arr	..	8 20	8 20	..	11 50	..	1 4	..	..	..	2 57	..	4 22	..	6 17	..	..	..	9 5	10 10	..	..	9 9	6 25
63	Cullompton	..	..	7 46	9 42	11 45	..	1 2	..	..	..	..	..	4 14	..	6 10	..	..	..	8 57	..	..	..	9 1	6 15
67	Hele and Bradninch	..	..	7 56	9 52	11 58	..	1 12	..	..	..	..	..	4 25	..	6 17	..	..	..	9 6	..	..	..	9 10	6 25
68½	Silverton..	..	..	8 1	9 57	12 4	..	..	..	..	..	..	..	4 32	..	6 22	..	..	..	..	..	..	..	9 14	6 30
72	Stoke Canon	..	..	8 10	10 7	12 15	..	..	..	..	..	..	..	4 43	..	6 31	..	..	..	9 21	..	..	..	9 21	6 38
75½	**EXETER** .. arrival about	2 50	8 27	8 20	10 17	12 30	..	1 30	..	..	..	3 10	..	4 52	4 0	6 43	..	..	..	9 35	10 20	11 0	2 50	9 35	6 50
	Exeter .. .. dep. "	3 0	8 40	8 40	10 30	..	..	1 55	..	..	..	3 20	..	5 0	4 10	6 55	..	..	..	..	10 25	..	3 0	9 45	7 0
128½	Plymouth .. arr. "	4 40	10 48	10 48	1 10	..	..	4 44	..	..	..	5 20	..	7 43	6 0	9 40	..	..	..	..	12 10	..	4 40	12 26	9 50

A Third Class from Paddington and all intermediate Stations at which the Train stops as far as Chippenham inclusive, to Exeter and certain Stations below.
B Third Class to Local Stations, Stations on the Devon and Somerset, Somerset and Dorset, South Devon, Cornwall and West Cornwall Lines Van Parcels conveyed by this Train.
C Third Class from Great Western to all Stations beyond Bristol at which the Train stops, except from Paddington to Exeter and Barnstaple.
D Third Class from Paddington and Reading only to Tiverton, Exeter, and to South Molton and Barnstaple (via Taunton), and to South Devon, Cornwall and West Cornwall Stations; also from Midland Line by Train leaving Birmingham at 6.50 a.m. to Truro and Falmouth.
S Slip Carriage detached at Bridgwater at 3.6 p.m.
E Third Class from certain Midland Stations to Bridgwater, Yeovil, Taunton and Exeter, and Stations on Somerset and Dorset Line.
***** Stops at Nailsea on Saturdays.
Y Slip Carriage detached at Yatton at 5.35 p.m.
M Third Class from Paddington to South Molton and Barnstaple.
X Horses and Carriages conveyed by these Trains.

Working timetable for August 1874 for down passenger trains.

WATCHET BRANCH.

UP

Miles	Stations.	Arr. A.M.	Dep. A.M.	Remarks.
	Minehead … …	…	…	Stops at Norton Siding when required.
1¼	Dunster … …	…	…	
3¼	Blue Anchor …	…	…	
5¾	Washford … …	…	…	
8	Watchet … …	…	6 0	
9½	Williton … …	6 5	6 10	
13	Stogumber … …	6 20	6 23	
15½	Crow. Heathfield	6 33	6 35	
19½	Bishop's Lydeard	6 47	6 57	
22½	Norton Fitzwarren	7 10	7 15	
24½	Taunton … …	7 20	…	

DOWN

Miles	Stations.	Arr. A.M.	Dep. A.M.	Remarks.
	Taunton … …	…	8 0	Stops at Norton Siding when required.
2	Norton Fitzwarren	…	8 5	
5	Bishop's Lydeard	8 10	8 15	
9	Crow. Heathfield	8 27	8 32	
11½	Stogumber … .	8 38	8 41	
15	Williton … …	8 48	8 52	
16½	Watchet … …	9 0	…	
18¾	Washford … …	…	…	
21	Blue Anchor …	…	…	
23	Dunster … …	…	…	
24¾	Minehead … …	…	…	

Working timetable for August 1874 for goods trains.

A week later the B&ER agreed to the new rates, but through 'a clerical error' omitted to issue them! They were:

	Miles	*Charge* *s. d.*	*Sidings* *d.*	*Total* *s. d.*
Watchet-Bishop's Lydeard	12	2 0	6	2 6
Watchet-Crowcombe	8	1 4	6	1 10
Watchet-Stogumber	6	1 0	6	1 6
Watchet-Williton	2	6	6	1 0

The WSR was concerned about these rates because there was no competition for coal being loaded at Dunball, Bridgwater and sent onwards by rail, and if charges were high, it would lose traffic to the other ports. In a letter of 28th June, 1869 J.C. Wall, the B&ER's General Manager, said that the rates charged from Watchet were the same proportionally as from Bridgwater. If rates from Watchet were reduced as the WSR proposed, a corresponding reduction would have to be made in rates from Bridgwater, so each railway company would suffer a loss. Wall said that the charges on the WSR did not exceed the B&ER's Parliamentary limit. As the WSR still pressed for lower charges, Wall said that he would recommend to his Directors that the matter should be submitted to arbitration 'by any Railway Manager you may select for us'.

William Forbes of 70 Bishopsgate Street, London, selected as arbitrator, and whom the WSR Directors said 'was a gentleman highly recommended for his thorough acquaintance with all the details of the general regulation of Railway Traffic Charges', sent his report of 19th December, 1869 to the WSR Directors. Forbes said that it was a misapprehension that coal rates were calculated on a certain sum per mile plus terminal charges; in practice they were governed by circumstances, the rule being 'to secure the best paying rates consistent with the full and fair development of the traffic of the Railway and its district'. The rates charged by the B&ER in November 1869 satisfied traders.

Forbes said that WSR traffic suffered through lack of a local agent with a lively interest in the development of the WSR's resources and proposed Mr Ford, harbourmaster at Watchet, be offered £20 per annum plus a commission of 1*d*. a ton on increased tonnage from station. Unfortunately the company's Minute books do not reveal whether this suggestion was adopted. Forbes urged the completion of the extension to Minehead.

On 8th March J.C. Wall sent the WSR a letter saying that as the WSR had not put in sidings at Norton Junction, coal to the west had to be hauled to Taunton before completing its journey, this double mileage being borne by the B&ER. He said that from 1st July, 1870 his company would charge this extra mileage unless the WSR laid sidings.

As the working agreement with the B&ER only allowed a payment of just over 2 per cent on the preference shares, nothing was left for ordinary shareholders. In 1870 a change was made on the guaranteed minimal rental paid by the B&ER to the WSR, an increase of £300 being made each year from £4,500 in 1870 to £6,600 in 1877. This latter payment continued until 1922, the final dividend being 4 per cent preference and 2¾ per cent on ordinary shares.

By an Act of 24th June, 1889 the redemption of the existing preference shares was authorised, new 4 per cent irredeemable preference shares being issued in lieu, powers also being granted for the raising of £10,000 by shares and £3,300 on loan. On 1st January, 1876 the B&ER had been taken over by the GWR, which absorbed the WSR as from 1st January, 1922, WSR stock being exchanged for GWR stock giving the same income:

WSR stocks		*GWR stocks issued in exchange*	
£40,000	4% debenture	£40,000	4% debenture
£76,200	4% debenture	£60,960	5% rent charge stock (£80 for each £100 WSR stock)
£67,780	Ordinary stock	£37,279	5% rent charge stock (£55 for each £100 WSR stock).

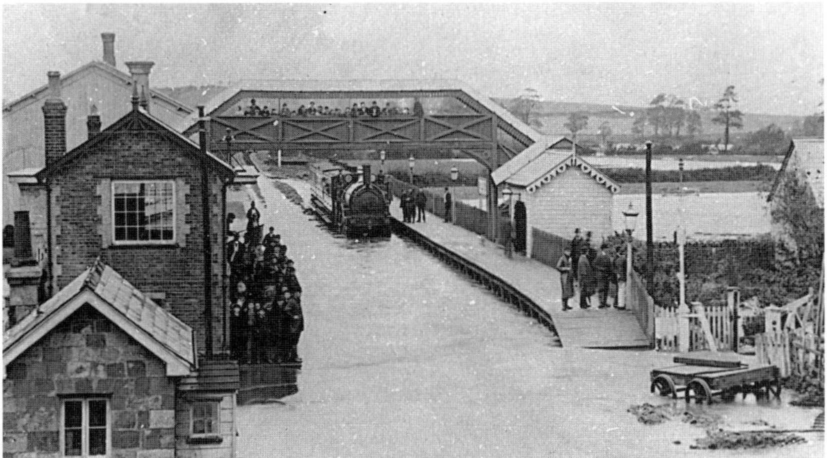

At the south end of Williton station the Doniford Stream is crossed by a bridge. Floods were not unknown. Here in 1877 a broad gauge 4-4-0ST is depicted hauling a 3-coach train. On the right can be seen a permanent way trolley. In the 1920s the covered timber footbridge was replaced by an open one in latticework. The up platform is of timber construction. *Author's Collection*

THE MINEHEAD RAILWAY

THE OPENING DAY

The introduction of a railway into any locality is, in these days of progress, commercial activity, and general desire for a quick method of travelling, an undertaking invariably frought with advantages to all classes of the public; and never have we heard of an instance in which the effect has been contrary to this . . . The district westward from Williton has for many years been one of the few strongholds of coaches, and the railway to Minehead being now completed and opened for traffic, eight miles of road will be deducted from their journeys . . .

The branch line joins the West Somerset Railway at Watchet and will be worked by the Bristol and Exeter Company. Its first sod was cut at Minehead on the 28th of December, 1871 . . .

Newspaper account from *West Somerset Free Press* of 18th July, 1874 of the opening of the Minehead Railway

Chapter Three

The Minehead Railway

When the WSR opened on 31st March, 1862, Watchet and Williton became the railheads for Minehead, but some thought that the line should be extended to Minehead itself. The first attempt at building a railway to Minehead was a plan for a standard gauge branch from the West Somerset Mineral Railway's main line* at Washford to the harbour at Minehead. Although an Act, 20 & 21 Vict. cap. 66 of 27th July, 1857 was secured, authorising a capital to be raised of £35,000 and £11,500 on loans to build a line from the WSMR at Washford, the idea was dropped when it became clear that Watchet Harbour alone would be adequate for shipping iron ore. In 1864 Henry Luttrell, and his nephew George Luttrell, of Dunster, were leading promoters of the Minehead Railway Company, which was to build a broad gauge line from an end-on junction with the WSR at Watchet.

The line was planned to run from Watchet to the south-west end of the pier at Minehead, not finishing near the beach as eventually built. It was intended that two miles of the standard gauge WSMR between Watchet and Washford would be changed to mixed gauge, but the WSMR opposed this plan and broad gauge rails were laid on WSMR land alongside the standard gauge line.

Before the Act was obtained, an agreement was made with the B&ER for it to work the line and in return 'The Minehead Company shall abstain from doing or concurring in anything that might directly or indirectly interrupt, hinder, interfere with, or in any way disturb the use, or quiet enjoyment by the Bristol Company, of any of the powers and privileges intended to be secured to them by this agreement'.

The Minehead Railway, with George Luttrell as Chairman, was granted an Act, 28 & 29 Vict. cap. 317 of 5th July, 1865 but the capital of £70,000 could not be raised. Unusually, this Act made no provision for the exercise of borrowing powers. In due course its powers lapsed and a new Act was obtained, 34 & 35 Vict. cap. 96 of 29th June, 1871, George Luttrell again being voted Chairman. The company was authorised to raise £60,000: £45,000 by preference shares class A and £15,000 by preference shares class B. It was intended that the Minehead Railway would cross the WSMR on the level at Watchet, but the mineral railway objected and a bridge over it was substituted.

The first meeting of the Directors was held at the Manor Offices, Dunster on 14th August, 1871 when it was resolved that tenders for the work would be obtained immediately. On 28th December, 1871 the contract of Frederick Furness to construct the line for £37,000, excluding stations, was accepted. Furness was later joined by a partner, William Buxton. Furness & Buxton sub-let the signalling contract to Hennet & Co., Bridgwater, who fitted Easterbrook & Co.'s equipment.

On 28th December, 1871, the first sod was cut on the same day that the contract was signed, the *West Somerset Free Press* recording:

---

* The West Somerset Mineral Railway was a standard gauge single line which ran 13 miles from Watchet to Gupworthy serving iron ore mines. It closed in 1898 but had a brief second life 1907-10; it was lifted in 1917.

Gradient Profile of the Minehead branch

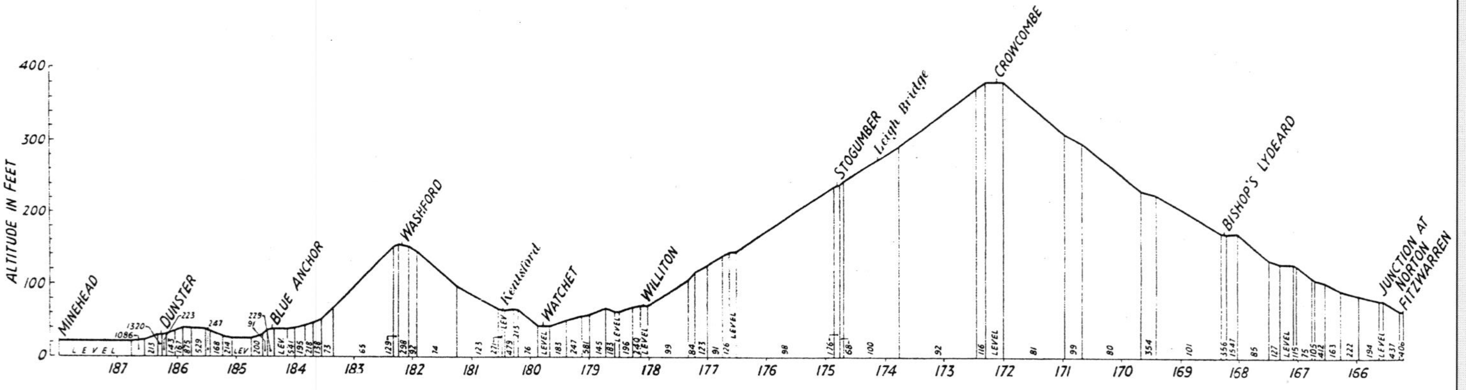

The first sod was cut on Thursday in last week. The town was decked with flags and a procession was formed which, headed by flags and the band, marched thro' Station-road to the site selected for the terminus.

Cannon were planted in a meadow near, from which were fired several salutes. Master Alexander Fownes Luttrell, eldest son of the Squire, cut the first sod, loaded the barrow, and wheeled it away in a workman-like manner. A similar act was performed by Mr G.F. Luttrell and others. The wheelbarrow and spade were presented to Master Luttrell as mementoes.

Loud cheers were given, volleys fired in the town, the band played at intervals, several tar barrels were ignited and rolled up and down, and the church bells were rung.

Tenders for building the stations were:

Date tender signed	*Contractor*	*Station*	*Amount*
27th May, 1872	William Harrison	Dunster	£912
27th May, 1872	John Pearse	Minehead	£1,118 17*s.* 6*d.*
8th August, 1872	William Morse	Washford	£940
2nd September, 1872	John Pearse	Blue Anchor	£350

All stations on the Minehead Railway had 400 ft-long platforms. Construction proceeded with few difficulties, apart from water in the deep cutting near Dragon Cross, just west of Washford.

The Board of Trade inspection was made on 13th July, 1874 by Capt F.H. Rich who reported:

Railway Department
Board of Trade
14th July, 1874

Sir,

In compliance with the instructions contained in your Minute of the 25th ultimate, I have the honour to report, for the information of the Board of Trade, that I have inspected the Minehead Railway, which extends from Watchet to Minehead.

The new line is 8 m. 75 ch. long and is single throughout with sidings. The guage [*sic*] is 7 ft and the intervals between the main line and the sidings are not less than 6 ft.

The permanent way consists of a Vignoles pattern rail that weighs 71 lbs per lineal yard. It is fished and fixed with fang bolts, to sleepers laid transversely at an average distance of 3 ft apart, except the sleepers next to the joints of the rails which are only 2 ft apart.

The sleepers are 11 ft long 10" x 5". The line is ballasted with gravel.

The stations are Watchet - where the new line joins the railway from Taunton to Watchet - Washford - Blue Anchor Bay, Dunster and Minehead. A turntable has been provided at the latter station.

There is an authorised level crossing of a public road at Blue Anchor Bay station. The gates close across the road and railway.

The steepest gradient is 1 in 66 and the sharpest curve has a radius of 12 chains.

The works consist of three bridges over and six bridges under the railway that are built of stone. One bridge over a mineral railway has wrought iron girders on stone abutments.

The following works require to be attended to - a skew bridge under the railway required to have the wing walls banked up.

The cutting between and Watchet station required to be trimmed off in places and to have a drain made into the field at the north side to carry off the water and protect it from soaking through into the cutting and causing the side to slip. This cutting should be watched.

MINEHEAD BRANCH.

NARROW GAUGE.

Single Line worked by Train Staff. The Staff Stations are Norton Fitzwarren, Williton, Watchet, and Minehead.

Section.	*Form of Staff and Tickets.*	*Colour of Ticket.*
Norton Fitzwarren and Williton	Square	Red.
Williton and Watchet	Triangular	White.
Watchet and Minehead	Round	Blue.

Down Trains. TAUNTON TO MINEHEAD. Week Days only.

Miles from Taunton	STATIONS.	1 Goods. arr.	1 Goods. dep.	2 Passenger. arr.	2 Passenger. dep.	3 Goods. arr.	3 Goods. dep.	4 Passenger. arr.	4 Passenger. dep.	5 Passenger. arr.	5 Passenger. dep.	6 Passenger. arr.	6 Passenger. dep.	7 Passenger. arr.	7 Passenger. dep.	8	8	9	9
		A.M.	A.M.	A.M.	A.M.	A.M.	A.M.	A.M.	A.M.	P.M.	P.M.	P.M.	P.M.	P.M.	P.M.				
	Taunton	....	6 20	....	8 0	....	10 5	....	11 30	....	1 55	**A**	4 10	....	7 0				
2	Norton Fitzwarren	6 26	6 40	8 4	8 5	10 11X	10 25	11 34	11 35	1 59	2 0	4 14	4 15	7 4	X7 5	....	....	....	....
2½	Norton Siding	—	—	—	—	C R		—	—	—	—	—	—	—	—	..	..	..	..
5	Bishop's Lydeard	6 55	7 5	8 14	8 15	10 40	10 48	11 44	11 45	2 7	2 8	4 24	4 25	7 14	7 15	....	....	....	....
9	Crowcombe	7 25	7 35	8 26	8 27	11 3	11 10	11 56	11 58	2 18	2 19	4 35	4 36	7 26	7 28	..	..	..	..
11¾	Stogumber	7 45	7 55	8 33	8 34	11 19	11 27	12 3	12 5	2 24	2 25	4 41	4 42	7 33	7 35	....	....	....	....
15	Williton	8 6	8 15	8 41	X8 43	•11 38	X12 25	•12 13	X12 16	2 31	X2 33	4 49	X4 51	7 42	X7 44	..	..	..	..
16¾	Watchet	X8 20	..	8 48	X8 49	12 32	12 39	12 19	12 20	2 38	2 39	4 55	4 56	7 48	7 49	....	....	....	....
19	Washford			8 55	8 56	12 47	12 52	12 26	12 27	2 45	2 46	5 2	5 3	7 55	7 56	..	..	..	..
21¼	Blue Anchor	..	..	9 2	9 3	—	—	12 32	12 33	2 51	2 52	5 9	5 10	8 1	8 2	....	....	....	....
23	Dunster	....	....	9 8	9 10	1 6	1 13	12 38	12 40	2 58	3 0	5 14	5 16	8 6	8 8	..	..	..	..
24¾	**Minehead**	..	..	9 15	..	1 20	..	12 45	..	3 5	..	5 20	..	8 13	..	....	....	....	....

A Runs on Saturdays only.

CROSSING ARRANGEMENTS BETWEEN NORTON FITZWARREN AND MINEHEAD.

The 6.20 a.m. Train from Taunton will cross the 8.10 a.m. Train from Minehead at Watchet.

The 8.0 a.m. Train from Taunton will cross the 8.10 a.m. Train from Minehead at Williton, and the 8.55 a.m. Train from Watchet at Watchet.

The 10.5 a.m. Train from Taunton will cross the 8.55 a.m. Train from Watchet at Norton Fitzwarren; the 11.45 a.m. Train from Minehead at Williton, and shunt for the 11.30 a.m. Train from Taunton, at Williton.

The 11.30 a.m. Train from Taunton will cross the 11.45 a.m. from Minehead, and pass the 10.5 a.m. Train from Taunton at Williton.

The 1.55 p.m. Train from Taunton will cross the 2.0 p.m. Train from Minehead at Williton.

The 4.10 p.m. Train from Taunton on Saturdays will cross the 3.40 p.m. Train from Minehead at Williton.

The 7.0 p.m. Train from Taunton will cross the 5.50 p.m. Train from Minehead at Norton Fitzwarren, and on Saturdays it will cross the 7.10 p.m. Train from Minehead at Williton.

Working timetable 1886.

Up Trains. **MINEHEAD TO TAUNTON.** **Week Days only.**

Miles from Minehead.	STATIONS.	1		2		3		4		5		6		7		8		9	
		Passenger.		**Goods.**		Passenger.		Passenger.		**Goods.**		Passenger.		**A** Passenger.					
		arr.	dep.	arr.	dep.	arr.	dep.	arr.	dep.	arr.	dep.	arr.	dep.	arr.	dep.				
		A.M.	A.M.	A.M.	A.M.	A.M.	A.M.	P.M.	P.M.	P.M.	P.M.	P.M.	P.M.	P.M.	P.M.				
	Minehead	....	8 10	....	....	....	11 45	....	2 0	....	3 40	....	5 50	....	7 10	....	....	....	....
1¾	Dunster	8 14	8 15	..	..	11 48	11 49	2 3	2 4	3 46	3 51	5 54	5 55	7 14	7 15	..	..	..	..
3½	Blue Anchor	8 20	8 21	....	....	11 54	11 55	2 9	2 10	—	—	6 0	6 1	7 20	7 21	....	....	....	....
5¾	Washford	8 28	8 29	..	..	12 3	12 4	2 17	2 18	4 5	4 10	6 8	6 9	7 28	7 29	..	..	..	..
8	Watchet	8 34	X8 36	....	X8 55	12 9	12 10	2 23	2 24	4 17	4 27	6 16	6 17	7 35	7 36	....	....	....	....
9¾	Williton	8 41	X8 44	9 0	9 5	12 15	X12 18	2 29	X2 32	4 32	X4 50	6 22	6 25	7 42	X7 44	..	..	..	..
13	Stogumber	8 52	8 54	9 14	9 20	12 26	12 27	2 39	2 40	4 59	5 4	6 33	6 34	7 52	7 53	....	....	....	....
15¾	Crowcombe	9 3	9 4	9 29	9 34	12 35	12 36	2 47	2 48	5 13	5 18	6 42	6 43	8 1	8 2	..	..	..	..
19¾	Bishop's Lydeard	9 12	9 13	9 44	9 49	12 42	12 43	2 53	2 54	5 28	5 33	6 49	6 50	8 8	8 9	....	....	....	....
22¼	Norton Siding	—	—	—	—	—	—	—	—	C.	R.	—	—	—	—	..	..	..	..
22¾	Norton Fitzwarren	9 22	9 24	9 59	X10 25	12 49	12 51	2 59	3 1	5 48	6 0	6 56	X6 58	8 14	8 17	....	....	....	....
24¾	**Taunton**	9 29	..	10 30	..	12 56	..	3 5	..	6 5	..	7 3	..	8 22	..	..	..	..	..

A Runs on Saturdays only.

CROSSING ARRANGEMENTS BETWEEN MINEHEAD AND NORTON FITZWARREN.

The 8.10 a.m. Train from Minehead will cross the 6.20 a.m. Train from Taunton at Watchet, and the 8.0 a.m. Train from Taunton at Williton.

The 8.55 a.m. Train from Watchet will cross the 8.0 a.m. Train from Taunton at Watchet, and the 10.5 a.m. Train from Taunton at Norton Fitzwarren.

The 11.45 a.m. Train from Minehead will cross the 10.5 a.m. and 11.30 a.m. Trains from Taunton at Williton.

The 2.0 p.m. Train from Minehead will cross the 1.55 p.m. Train from Taunton at Williton.

The 3.40 p.m. Train from Minehead will cross the 4.10 p.m. Train from Taunton on Saturdays at Williton.

The 5.50 p.m. Train from Minehead will cross the 7.0 p.m. Train from Taunton at Norton Fitzwarren.

The 7.10 p.m. Train from Minehead on Saturdays will cross the 7.0 p.m. Train from Taunton at Williton.

Working timetable 1886.

What appears to be a broad gauge 2-2-2 at Minehead station *c.* 1880. Notice the disc and crossbar signal - the crossbar indicating 'Danger'. *Author's Collection*

Minehead station *c.* 1900. *Author's Collection*

A guard rail is required on the 12 chain curve at the West side of the bridge over the mineral railway.

The locking bars for the facing points on this passenger line are on the ground, but they require to be fixed.

The points at Dunster require adjusting and the Up station signal requires to be locked with the siding points.

The engineer [Mr Dennis] has promised to have these two items completed at once and I submit that the Board of Trade may sanction the opening of the Minehead Railway.

I have etc.
F.H. Rich

PS I enclose a document of the undertaking of the mode in which the railway is to be worked, which appears satisfactory. The yard of the Bristol & Exeter Railway Co. at Watchet is not fenced off from what appears to be a public road to the quay. The company should be reminded that this is necessary. The Bristol & Exeter Co. has leased the Minehead Railway and are to work it.

The line opened to the public on 16th July, 1874, the first up train leaving Minehead at 6.00 am returning as the 7.45 am ex-Taunton with 200 passengers. The 11.05 am ex-Taunton brought 800 passengers including company Directors and officials of the B&ER. Minehead was decorated, there were five arches and firs were planted at the roadside. Church bells rang at Minehead and there were flags at Dunster. Luncheon was held in a tent erected on ground between the station and the beach. The following day Furness & Buxton used the same tent for treating 160 navvies to dinner and beer.

As with the WSR, the line was worked by the B&ER for a rental of not less than £2,000 per annum and when gross receipts exceeded £4,000, 50 per cent of the gross receipts. On 23rd January, 1875 the Directors instructed Dennis to certify completion of works as soon as the fencing from Minehead to Dunster was finished.

An interesting and amusing letter appeared in the *West Somerset Free Press* of 13th November, 1875 and in view of the fact that it was written only five years after the Education Act of 1870 was passed, and until then only one in three children attended school, the correspondent had a valid criticism.

Sir

In the *Free Press* about a month ago, it was stated that '*third* class tickets would be issued by all trains from Minehead to all local stations, and *vice versa*'. That *vice versa* puzzled me a bit. 'What does that French or Greek stuff mean?' I asked a stationmaster. 'T'aint French or Greek, but Latin', he said, and looked uncommon knowing. 'What does it mean then?' 'I'm blessed if I can *exactly* tell you; but I think it means the *reverse*, or back again'.

Bless their crabbed Latin stuff; why they want to use that about third class trains and not about first class ones I can't think. I can understand school boards wanting to teach Latin; but why railway boards and boards at railway stations are used for that purpose I can't imagine.

If the Company again use Latin to guide third class passengers, I hope they will use Chinese for the first class and double Dutch for the second, as that would put us on an equal-footing.

Penny-A-Miler

The Minehead Railway was absorbed by the GWR from 1st July, 1897 by which time that company had acquired all its capital.

Watchet Harbour *c.* 1870; the crossbar of a disc and crossbar signal is evident.

Courtesy: H.H. Hole

B&ER 4-4-0T No. 74 on the turntable at Watchet *c.* 1870. No. 74, built in 1867, became GWR No. 2047 and lasted until the end of the broad gauge in May 1892. The crew are wearing white fustian uniform. To work the table, they stood on the platform set down in the pit and turned the crank on the left. The left hand wagon is No. 551 and part of No. 131 appears between the two wagons in the foreground. The left hand wagon of the pair in the background has curved ends and appear to be No. 537. *Courtesy: H.H. Hole*

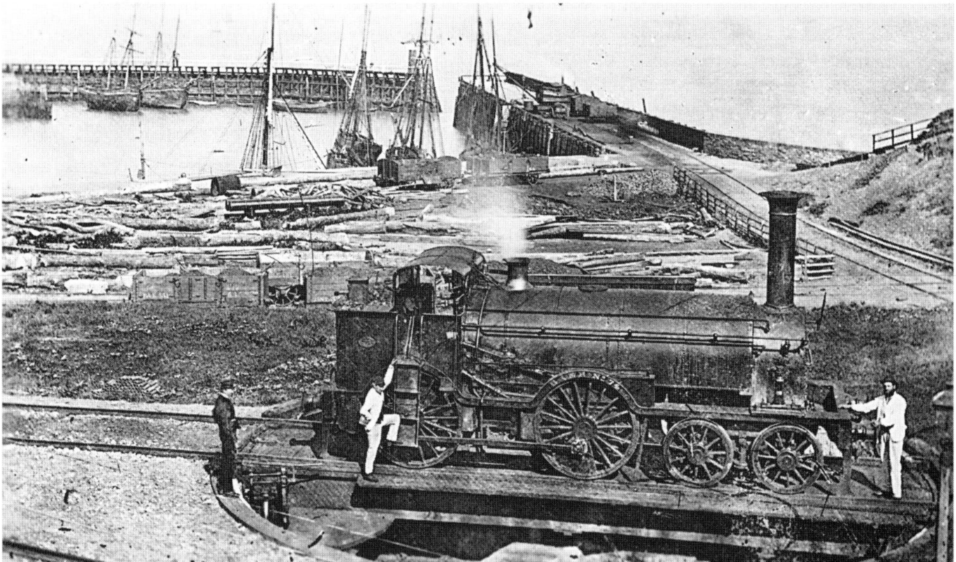

Chapter Four

Watchet Harbour

In 1857, the same year as the WSR Act was passed, Watchet Harbour was vested in Commissioners, these undertaking to improve the harbour according to plans laid out by the late Rice Hopkins. In order to protect its interests, the WSR had the right to appoint a Commissioner. About the time the WSR was being planned, a 590 ft-long East pier of stone and timber had been built to protect the harbour from easterly winds, the original jetty only protecting vessels from the prevailing westerlies. The beach at the end of the pier was turned into a wharf. The loss of this sandy beach was greatly regretted by local children and visitors. The problem of infilling the land behind the newly-built wharf wall was solved by selling this area between the wall and the WSR to that company for £50 on condition it was raised level. The Harbour Commissioners retained at the edge of the wharf a parcel of land and 30 ft in width for their use. Lack of funds prevented the Commissioners carrying out their full development scheme, including a floating harbour.

William Forbes' report of 19th December, 1869 (*see page 16*), explained details of railway working at the harbour. In the autumn of 1867 Thomas Griffiths offered to provide and work a steam crane for unloading coal from vessels into railway wagons and moving them from the East Pier to the WSR's main line. His offer was accepted by the Harbour Commissioners, though actually it was not within their province to provide and pay for hauling wagons to the main line at Watchet, which should rightly have been performed by the B&ER at the latter's cost. However, the arrangement was unchallenged until Griffiths demanded of the B&ER a further 2*d.* per ton and in November 1869 the B&ER agreed, he thus received double payment for one service! Forbes said that as Griffiths had volunteered to work at 6*d.* a ton and negotiated with the B&ER to do so, he should have kept to his agreement. The charge for unloading coal from vessels into wagons should have been 4*d.* at Watchet, the same as Bridgwater. Hauling to the main line at both these places was performed and paid for by the B&ER. At one time Bridgwater charges were set low to compete with Dunball, the latter then being in private hands, but as both were now owned by the B&ER, this no longer applied.

Freight charges by sea for pitwood from Watchet was 6*d.* to 8*d.* a ton less than from Bridgwater. J.C. Wall the B&ER's General Manager said he was always ready to grant a special rate for this traffic from WSR stations to Watchet proportionate to the Bridgwater special rates, but no application had been made.

Special rates for pitwood to Bridgwater:

From	*Charge per ton*	*From*	*Charge per ton*
	s. d.		*s. d.*
Bishop's Lydeard	1 9	Stogumber	2 0
Crowcombe	1 9	Williton	2 0

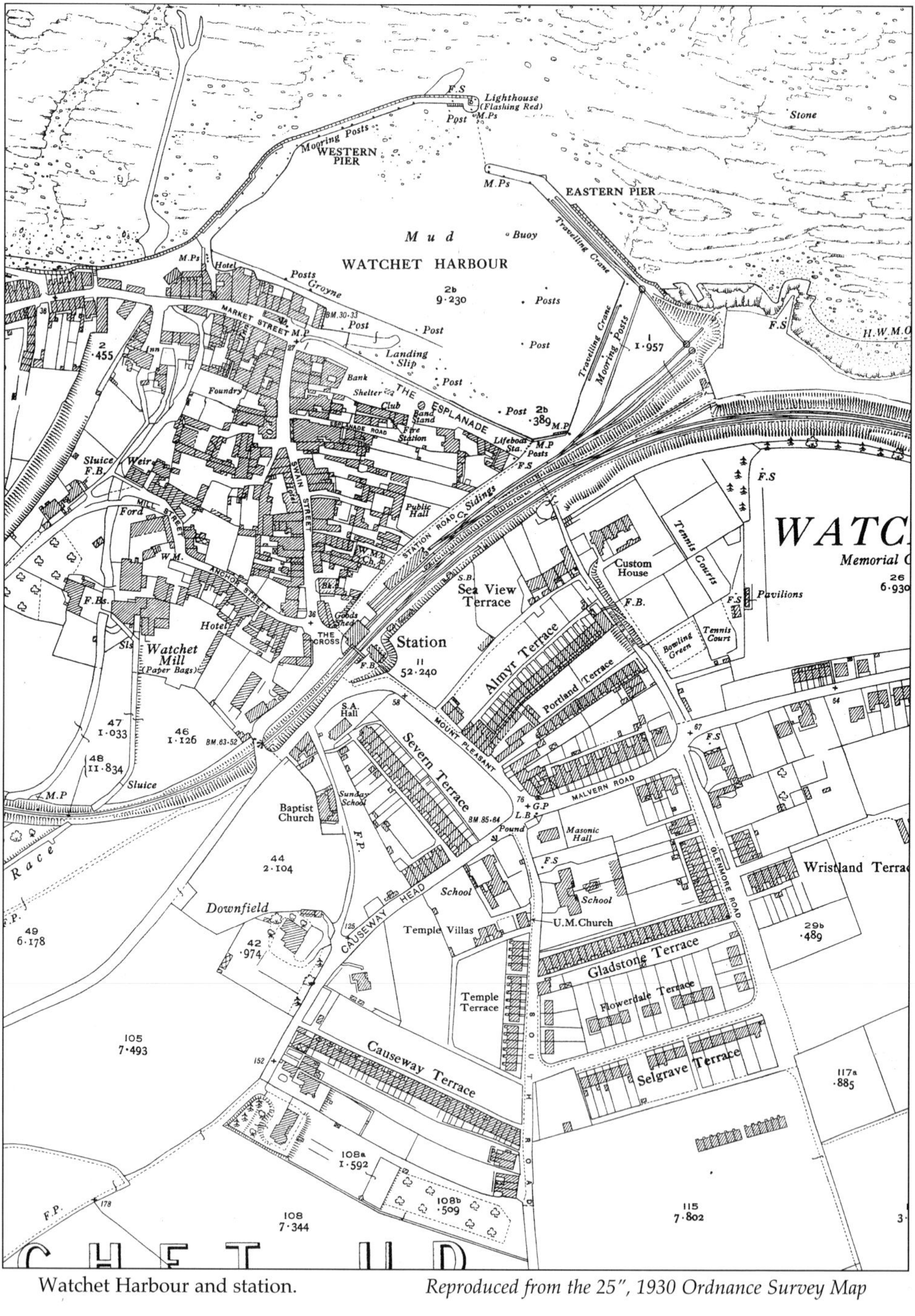

Watchet Harbour and station. *Reproduced from the 25", 1930 Ordnance Survey Map*

Forbes said that the coal import trade at Watchet was injured by a lack of sufficient wagons, but Bridgwater suffered the same scarcity. In consequence of the impossibility of guaranteeing wagons at Watchet or Bridgwater, coal was sent to Exeter via Fremington and the North Devon Railway, thus being a loss to the WSR and the B&ER. Although the B&ER was increasing its wagon fleet, Watchet would continue to be at a serious disadvantage compared with Bridgwater until private owners' wagons were provided as at Bridgwater. The B&ER made an allowance of an eighth of a penny per ton/mile to traders providing their own wagons and was ready to extend the same rebate to WSR traders.

Shunting on the harbour lines was by horse. No direct run could be made from the jetty to the GWR and one of the three wagon turntables had to be negotiated.

Termination of railway goods traffic in the 1960s meant that land which the Harbour Commissioners had sold to the railway in 1861 for £50, was repurchased, together with a small goods shed and a long strip of land adjacent to Harbour Road, for £10,000.

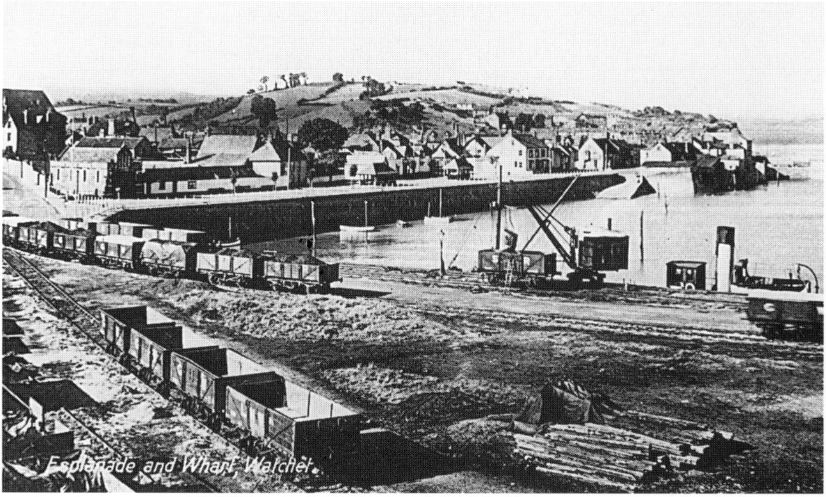

Watchet *c.* 1925 showing the harbour sidings. There is an LNWR wagon in the foreground, but the rest of the wagons are in post-grouping livery.

Paul Strong Collection

MAP SHOWING THE PROPOSED RAILWAYS BETWEEN BRIDGWATER, STOGURSEY AND WATCHET

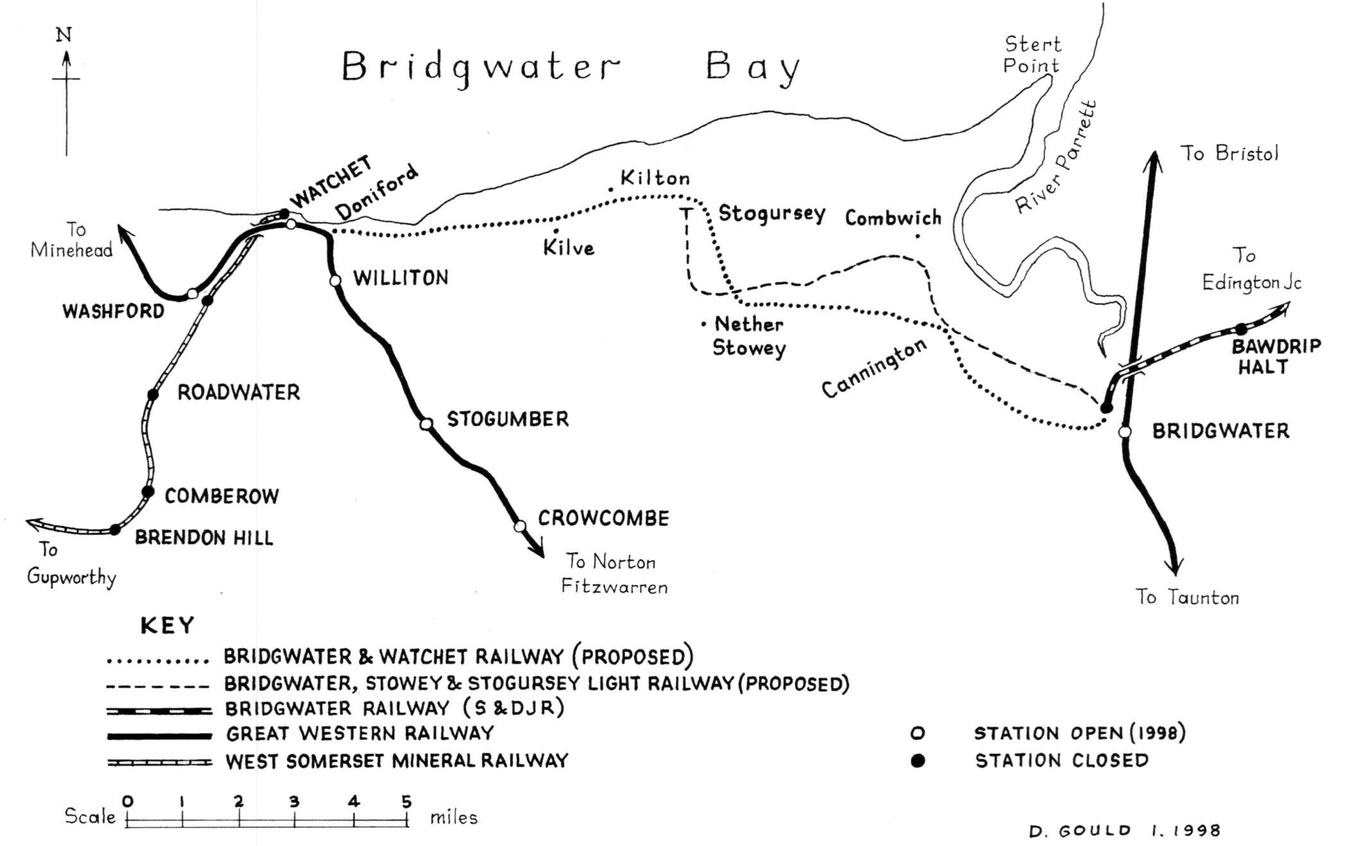

Chapter Five

Later History of the Branch

In 1882 a standard gauge line was proposed to run from the projected Somerset & Dorset Railway's branch at Bridgwater to Watchet where it was to link with the GWR and WSMR. Not unnaturally, the GWR strongly opposed this rival, describing it as 'tainted with the mark of the speculator'. Although supported by local landowners, the Bill was withdrawn, as was a similar application in the 1884 Session as there was no hope of raising the required capital of almost half a million pounds.

A comparable line was proposed in February 1899 when local inhabitants suggested to the London & South Western Railway that its proposed Bridgwater, Stowey & Stogursey Light Railway be extended to Watchet and continue via the WSMR to Exeter. Even into the 20th century a Bridgwater to Watchet line seemed attractive and a few years after Grouping the GWR proposed that to reduce unemployment, the Government could finance such a line.

In 1898 the Minehead & Lynmouth Light Railway was promoted. It was to have started at Minehead Harbour, but this proposal was dropped when strongly opposed by the town. From a terminus near the GWR's Minehead station, the narrow gauge line was to pass through the Vale of Porlock and swing towards the coast. From County Gate to Lynmouth it paralleled the present A39 road to a terminus above the village.

Sir George Newnes, a Director of the Lynton & Barnstaple Railway and newspaper magnate, ran a campaign against the Lynmouth & Minehead Railway claiming it would spoil Exmoor and ruin the stag hunting. Opposition also came from landowners and the National Trust.

A summary of the inquiry before the Light Railway Commissioners was reported in the *West Somerset Free Press* on 13th August, 1898.

> Proposal for a 2 ft gauge railway from Minehead adjoining the GWR terminus to Lynmouth; estimated cost, £87,000. The promoters were some of the Directors of the Barry Railway. It was really a South Wales scheme to bring excursionists by boat from Cardiff to Minehead and then by rail to Lynmouth. Distance, Minehead to Lynmouth 20 miles 3 furlongs. The steepest gradient proposed was 1 in 40. The only local supporter of standing was Mr G.F. Luttrell of Dunster Castle, who was a large owner of property in and about Minehead. The Engineer was Sir James Szlumper, who had been Consulting Engineer of the Lynton & Barnstaple Railway.
>
> After sitting for one day only, the Commissioners stated on the following morning that they saw no reason for prolonging the Enquiry; they could not recommend that compulsory powers should be exercised for the acquisition of land. It was purely a line for tourist traffic and would not help agricultural interests in the district.

Prior to, and after World War I Minehead had a Territorial summer camp on North Hill above the town. Apart from men, horses, field guns, limbers and other supplies arrived there by rail.

Traffic on the branch was halted for a few days during the General Strike in May 1926. At its beginning, 50 empty wagons were ready at Watchet for

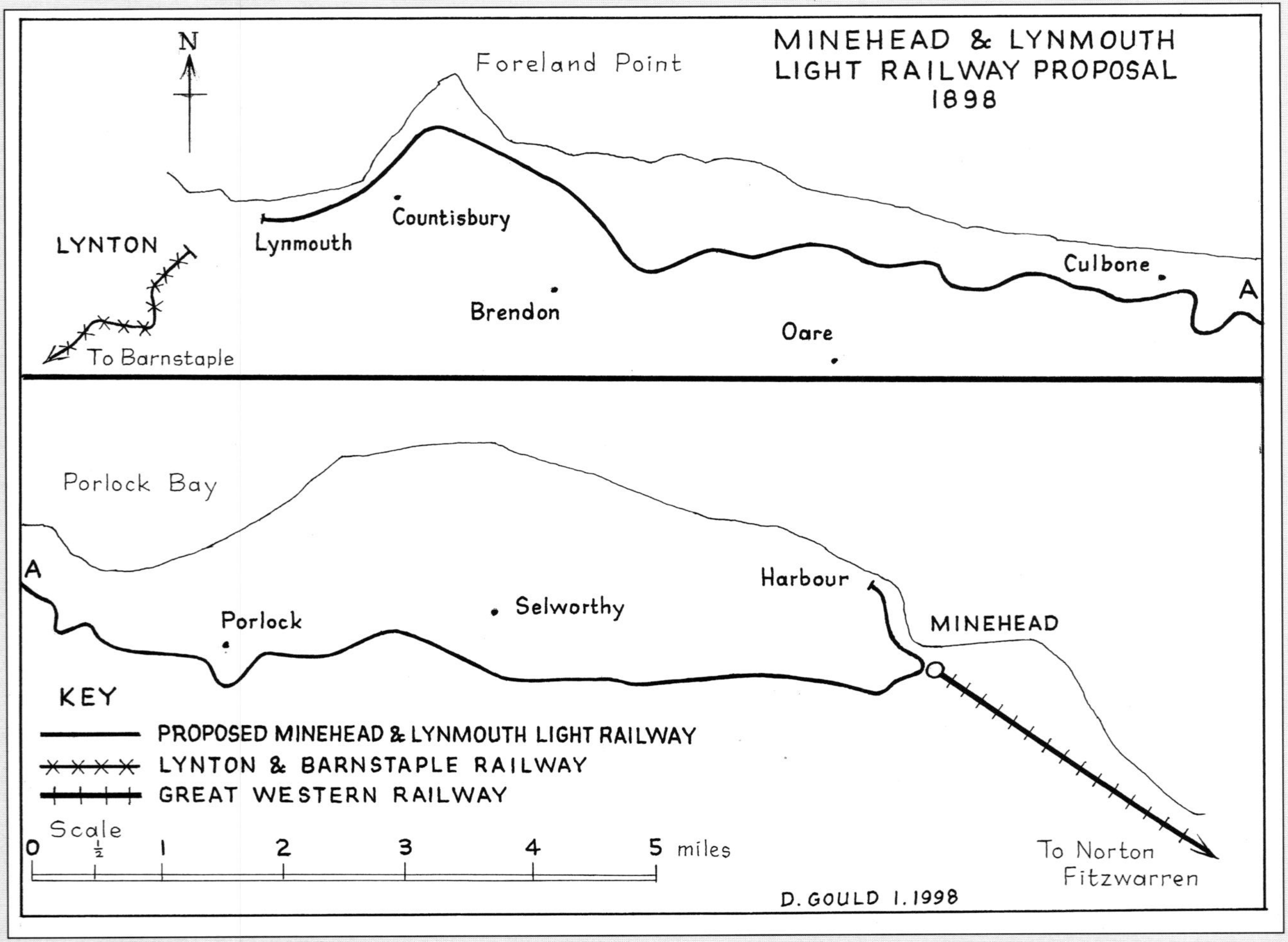
MINEHEAD & LYNMOUTH
LIGHT RAILWAY PROPOSAL
1898
N
Foreland Point
LYNTON
Lynmouth
Countisbury
Brendon
Oare
Culbone
A
To Barnstaple
Porlock Bay
A
Porlock
Selworthy
Harbour
MINEHEAD
KEY
PROPOSED MINEHEAD & LYNMOUTH LIGHT RAILWAY
LYNTON & BARNSTAPLE RAILWAY
GREAT WESTERN RAILWAY
Scale
0 ½ 1 2 3 4 5 miles
To Norton Fitzwarren
D. GOULD 1.1998

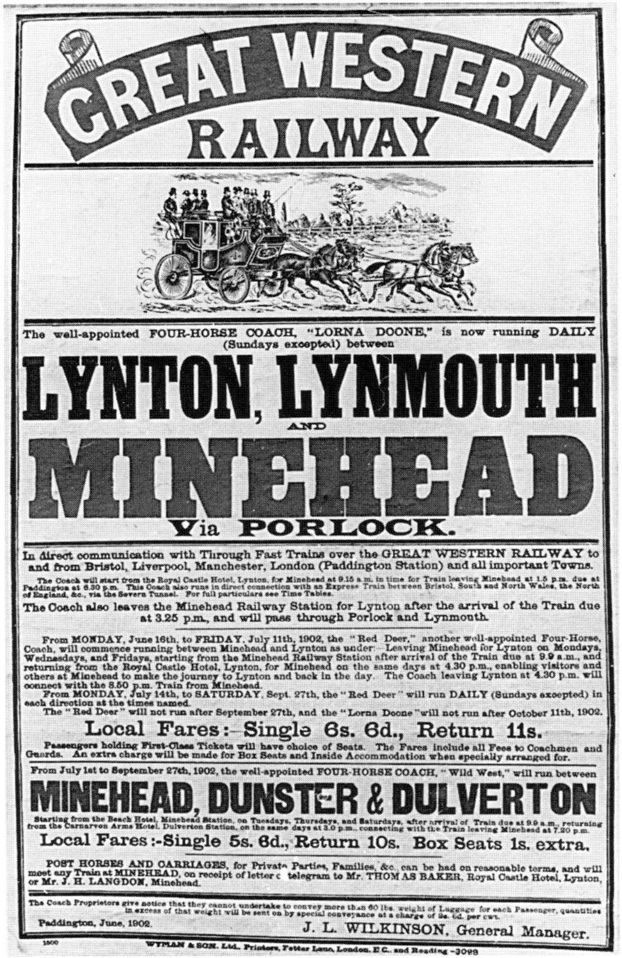

GREAT WESTERN
RAILWAY
The well-appointed FOUR-HORSE COACH, "LORNA DOONE," is now running DAILY (Sundays excepted) between
LYNTON, LYNMOUTH
AND
MINEHEAD
Via PORLOCK.
In direct communication with Through Fast Trains over the GREAT WESTERN RAILWAY to and from Bristol, Liverpool, Manchester, London (Paddington Station) and all important Towns.
The Coach will start from the Royal Castle Hotel, Lynton, for Minehead at 9.15 a.m. in time for Train leaving Minehead at 1.5 p.m. due at Paddington at 6.30 p.m. This Coach also runs in direct connection with an Express Train between Bristol, South and North Wales, the North of England, &c., via the Severn Tunnel. For full particulars see Time Tables.
The Coach also leaves the Minehead Railway Station for Lynton after the arrival of the Train due at 3.25 p.m., and will pass through Porlock and Lynmouth.
From MONDAY, June 16th, to FRIDAY, July 11th, 1902, the "Red Deer," another well-appointed Four-Horse, Coach, will commence running between Minehead and Lynton as under:—Leaving Minehead for Lynton on Mondays, Wednesdays, and Fridays, starting from the Minehead Railway Station after arrival of the Train due at 9.9 a.m., and returning from the Royal Castle Hotel, Lynton, for Minehead on the same days at 4.30 p.m., enabling visitors and others at Minehead to make the journey to Lynton and back in the day. The Coach leaving Lynton at 4.30 p.m. will connect with the 8.50 p.m. Train from Minehead.
From MONDAY, July 14th, to SATURDAY, Sept. 27th, the "Red Deer" will run DAILY (Sundays excepted) in each direction at the times named.
The "Red Deer" will not run after September 27th, and the "Lorna Doone" will not run after October 11th, 1902.
Local Fares:—Single 6s. 6d., Return 11s.
Passengers holding First-Class Tickets will have choice of Seats. The Fares include all Fees to Coachmen and Guards. An extra charge will be made for Box Seats and Inside Accommodation when specially arranged for.
From July 1st to September 27th, 1902, the well-appointed FOUR-HORSE COACH, "Wild West," will run between
MINEHEAD, DUNSTER & DULVERTON
Starting from the Beach Hotel, Minehead Station, on Tuesdays, Thursdays, and Saturdays, after arrival of Train due at 9.9 a.m., returning from the Carnarvon Arms Hotel, Dulverton Station, on the same days at 3.0 p.m., connecting with the Train leaving Minehead at 7.20 p.m.
Local Fares:-Single 5s. 6d., Return 10s. Box Seats 1s. extra.
POST HORSES AND CARRIAGES, for Private Parties, Families, &c., can be had on reasonable terms, and will meet any Train at MINEHEAD, on receipt of letter or telegram to Mr. THOMAS BAKER, Royal Castle Hotel, Lynton, or Mr. J. H. LANGDON, Minehead.
The Coach Proprietors give notice that they cannot undertake to convey more than 60 lbs. weight of Luggage for each Passenger, quantities in excess of that weight will be sent on by special conveyance at a charge of 2s. 6d. per cwt.
Paddington, June, 1902.
J. L. WILKINSON, General Manager.
1800
WYMAN & SON, Ltd., Printers, Fetter Lane, London, E.C., and Reading -3098

Left: GWR poster promoting the 4-horse Lorna Doone coach service to Lynton and Lynmouth dated June 1902.

Above: From 1st July, 1908 until 31st October, 1908 the GWR ran buses from Bridgwater to Holford and Kilve to cover the area north of the Minehead branch. The service was not a financial success. Here driver Hancock is at the wheel of 20 hp Milnes-Daimler AF 138, fleet No. 20.

Author's Collection

Horses and hounds of the Quantock Stag Hunt are seen as they arrive by rail at Minehead station.

carrying part of the cargo of woodpulp from the SS *Bojan* to Hele & Bradninch station, on the GWR main line between Tiverton Jn and Exeter, and when these were filled, the remainder of the pulp was left on the East Pier.

On 19th December, 1930 Geoffrey Luttrell, a descendant of the Luttrells who had been very active in the early history of the Minehead Railway, was appointed to the GWR Board of Directors and it was due to pressure from him that the branch was improved in the 1930s. Two extra crossing loops at Leigh Bridge and Kentsford broke up long sections; Dunster to Minehead was doubled, as was Bishop's Lydeard to Norton Fitzwarren, while station platforms were extended as were station crossing loops with improved track layouts for 40 mph running speeds. Eight '45XX' class 2-6-2Ts were equipped with electric train token exchanging apparatus allowing exchange at speeds up to the new 40 mph limit. All this amounted to a significant investment that greatly improved the working capacity of the line.

The Minehead branch was important from the military aspect. Doniford Camp east of Watchet, was a tented camp used in the 1920s and 1930s for training Royal Artillery territorial units, mainly from London. Every fortnight the railway brought new occupants, together with some of their equipment. On these change-over weekends, GWR road motor drivers from Taunton with their vehicles were used to assist moving the equipment. They considered this job a good 'perk' as they were 'fed and watered' at the sergeants' mess and housed overnight in a tent.

A small bi-plane towed a drogue target to give 'Territorials' shooting practice. The sound of gunfire was followed by a puff of smoke in the vicinity of the target. Later in the 1930s a radio-controlled 'Queen Bee' aircraft drew the target. On one memorable occasion when Leslie Hore-Belisha, Secretary of State for War 1937-40 visited the camp, the lads excelled themselves and shot down the 'Queen Bee'. During World War II Doniford Camp became a permanent site with bricks and mortar, and eventually married quarters. In the late 1940s and 1950s the camp was taken over by the RAF: the Army returning in 1957. The camp site is now a holiday centre.

In 1938 the threatening European situation caused the War Department to purchase Norton Manor Estate for conversion into a training camp for miltary personnel. As the camp site was only 1½ miles from Norton Fitzwarren station, materials and equipment needed for the construction arrived there, but heavier goods requiring cranage used Taunton Yard. The camp opened in 1939 to take one of the first contingents of peace-time conscripts. Prior to the outbreak of War in September 1939, these Royal Artillery lads practised using searchlights and detectors to locate aircraft.

It is recorded that with the commencement of air raids on London in August 1940, 750 to 800 evacuees from Lambeth arrived at Williton station to be billetted on local residents. Only 200 were expected, but all were found homes by the early hours. Other stations along the line probably received other evacuees. In 1944, prior to the D-Day Normandy landing, thousands of troops were stationed in the woods between Bishop's Lydeard and Stogumber, many arriving and departing by train.

Just after D-Day, special dispensation was granted to allow '28XX' class 2-8-0

Evacuees from London arriving at Williton during the first week of World War II. *Courtesy: H.H. Hole*

'4575' class 2-6-2T stands at Minehead awaiting departure with the 10.50 am for Taunton, 5th September, 1960. *Tom Heavyside*

'43XX' class 2-6-0 No. 6323 enters Watchet with an up express, 21st July, 1957. Notice that the station building stands at right angles to the platform. The goods shed is on the right.
N.C. Simmons

'5101' class 2-6-2T No. 4128 passes the camping coaches at Blue Anchor as it heads the 2.15 pm for Minehead, 19th August, 1962. *S.A. Leleux*

No. 2822 to run to Minehead to collect a train of ten Sherman tanks. These vehicles had been used in the area for training and were *en route* for Normandy. One night they were loaded end-on at the bay platform and the train left at 4 am. As No. 2822 was too long for the Minehead turntable, it ran tender-first.

Some soldiers tried to avoid paying for a travel ticket and at times a railwayman was sent from Taunton to Norton Fitzwarren armed with an excess ticket pad in order to catch these miscreants.

Peak summer Saturdays occurred in the 1950s when about 2,100 passengers arrived at Minehead. On 10th September, 1962 the branch was dieselised. In late December of that year when blizzards blocked roads between Taunton and Minehead, a snowplough cleared the railway. Points and signals were kept free of snow, while salt was used to prevent freezing. When drifts blocked the sidings at Watchet Harbour, troops from Doniford Camp set to work shovelling the snow away so that the esparto grass could be removed from a ship. Goods depots along the Minehead branch were kept busy as traffic during the 'Big Freeze' switched from road to rail. On 3rd January, 1963 the 1.21 pm ex-Taunton ploughed into a deep drift between Doniford and Williton. Troops could not dig it out and eventually a steam engine from Taunton hauled the dmu back to Wiilliton. A blizzard on 5th February blocked the line and after clearance by snowplough, the first train of the day arrived at Minehead at about 2.30 pm. Throughout the freeze the branch was staffed 24 hours a day and passenger receipts increased by 50 per cent.

The Beeching Report of 1963 recommended closure of the line and it was decided to withdraw traffic as soon as alternative bus services could be provided. By the mid-1960s the weekly average of 4,850 passengers on the branch, boosted by tourists, particularly to and from Butlin's Holiday Camp, to 5,000 per day on the peak summer Saturdays, did not provide sufficient revenue to make the line viable. Annual costs were:

	£
Movement	63,000
Terminal	20,000
Track and signalling	82,000
Interest and administration	18,000
Total cost	183,000
Less earnings	42,000
Total grant required	141,000

These figures were based on a formula which took no account of contributory revenue while true engineering costs were ignored and replaced by a high 'average' figure.

From 26th February, 1968 conductor/guards were provided economising in staff, as, except at terminal stations, passengers obtained their tickets on the train. By 1970 the number of staff employed at the branch stations had declined to 11 from approximately 55 in 1938.

Following a public hearing at Minehead, the Transport Users' Consultative Committee (South Western Area) issued this press statement on 2nd January, 1969:

A 3-car dmu passes the 187½ mile post working the 11.25 am *en route* for Taunton on 17th September, 1964. To the right can be seen Butlin's Holiday Camp which brought considerable traffic to the branch. *R.E. Toop*

A 6-coach train bound for Minehead leaves Crowcombe on 25th August, 1965 headed by a B-B type 2 'D63XX' North British diesel-hydraulic. The loading bank, principally used for stone, can be seen on the left. *Derrick Payne*

British Railways Board's Proposal to Withdraw the Passenger Train Service from Taunton-Minehead Line

The committee have considered the Board's proposal as above in conjunction with all the written representations received and oral evidence given at a public Hearing held at Minehead on 28th November, 1968.

The Committee are of the opinion that implementation of the proposal would cause considerable hardship to all users of the passenger train service during the summer holiday season.

They are also of the view that holidaymakers now visiting Minehead and West Somerset by rail would not or could not continue to do so if the trains were taken off. This would have an adverse effect on the economy and trade of the area, especially at Minehead, and hardship would result to many who depend on the holiday trade for their livelihood.

Some hardship would also be caused to users at out-of-season times and this would occur in varying degrees, but especially to those who use the trains for travelling to Taunton for their education and to work.

The Committee are unable to suggest means of alleviating the hardship if the train service is closed.

A comprehensive report has been submitted to the Minister of Transport.

The Pithay,
Bristol.

BR announced that the branch would close on 6th January, 1969, but as objections were raised, closure was deferred. Further economies were made on 1st March, 1970 when Bishop's Lydeard and Norton Fitzwarren signal boxes were closed, down trains crossing to their own line at Silk Mill signal box a mile west of Taunton and continuing to Bishop's Lydeard on the former up track, as the branch was singled from Norton Fitzwarren to Bishop's Lydeard.

On 19th March, 1970 the Ministry of Transport gave consent to close the line.

I am directed by the Minister of Transport to refer to the report of the Transport Users' Consultative Committee for the South Western Area upon objections and representations relating to the proposal to discontinue all railway passenger services between Taunton and Minehead.

The Minister accepts the view of the Committee that the closure would cause hardship to users of the line during the summer holiday period. During the remaining months of the year, however, he considers that the existing and some additional bus services could provide reasonable public transport facilities. The proportion of holidaymaker travelling to the area by rail has been estimated at about one-fifth, and the numbers using other forms of transport are rising every year.

Against the possibility of the occurrence of some hardship, the Minister has had to set the fact that the service is incurring a loss which, if it were to be met by a grant under Section 39 (1) of the Transport Act, 1963, would involve a grant of about £141,000 per annum. Having paid due regard to all the matters which appear to him to be relevant, including the social and economic considerations, the Minister has reluctantly decided that he should give his consent to the closure, but subject to the provision of certain additional bus services for all the year round travellers.

Bus services were not really a satisfactory alternative as they took twice as long as a train and even longer with road congestion in the summer. The

Circa 1966 an unidentified 'Hymek' diesel-hydraulic works an up train of about eight coaches at Washford. *Derrick Payne*

'Hymek' diesel-hydraulic No. D7026 leaves Blue Anchor with the 10.25 am Saturdays-only, Minehead to Paddington train on 18th July, 1970. *Hugh Ballantyne*

'additional bus services' were not immediately forthcoming and on 5th September, 1970 the *West Somerset Free Press* reported:

> The Taunton-Minehead branch line, due to close in a month's time, was given at least a temporary reprieve by the Western Area Traffic Commissioners at Taunton on Thursday.
>
> When the Minister of Transport agreed to the closure of the line he ordered that this should not take effect until there are adequate bus services.
>
> The Commissioners, after an all-day hearing, decided that mainly because of staffing problems, the [Bus] Company's proposals did not meet the Minister's requirements, and the application was adjourned *sine die*.
>
> A spokesman for the Company said later that this would mean that the line could not be closed for some months at least.

Closure eventually took place from Monday 4th January, 1971. BR made several workings after official closure, the first being on 3rd January, 1971 when a 'Hymek' collected the camping coaches from Blue Anchor. In 1971-72 rakes of 'Vanfits' were stored on the branch while in 1973 movements were made in the Crowcombe to Stogumber section in connection with filming 'The Belstone Fox'. In the week prior to the removal of No. 6229 *Duchess of Hamilton* from Butlin's Holiday Camp, Minehead, on 13th March, 1975, BR type 2 class '25' No. 25 029 ran over the branch to assess the line's condition. No. 6229 was hauled to Swindon Works for overhaul prior to being exhibited at the National Railway Museum, York.

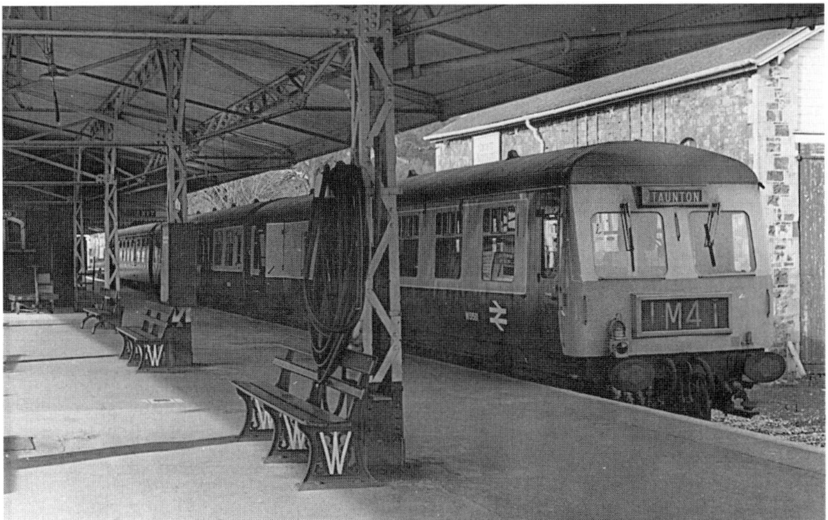

Swindon Works 3-car cross-country dmu with motor brake composite No. W51581 leading, stands at the main platform ready to return to Taunton on 1st February, 1968. The goods shed is in the background. Notice that the fall pipe from the canopy guttering comes neatly under the roof before being led down inside a support pillar.

W.H. Harbor/Author's Collection

The decorated Bagnall 0-6-0ST No. 2996 *Victor* runs around its train at Williton after arriving with the first WSR train from Minehead on 28th August, 1976. *Revd Alan Newman*

Park Royal 2-car dmu consisting of motor brake second No. 50413 and driving trailer composite No. 56168 leaves Blue Anchor with the 9.45 am Stogumber to Minehead train on 1st June, 1978. *Author*

Chapter Six

Re-birth of the Branch by the new West Somerset Railway

When it became clear that the Minehead branch would be closed, steps were taken to form a new company to buy the line from the British Railways Board (BRB) and re-open it running a commuter service to Taunton. BRB set a price of £245,000, plus £6,000 a year for running powers over its tracks between Norton Fitzwarren and Taunton. The West Somerset Railway Company Limited, quite unconnected with the former company of this name, was incorporated on 5th May, 1971. After discussions, Somerset County Council agreed to purchase the line and lease it to the WSR.

An inquiry was held in the Shire Hall, Taunton on 22nd January, 1974 regarding objections to a Light Railway Order being granted, these being raised by the Western National Omnibus Company, the Disused Railways Action Group, Mr Guy Somerset and Mr A.G. Liebert. Somerset County Council (SCC) proposed making a loan of £60,000 to the WSR and offering a subsidy of £10,000 for two years by reducing the rent on condition that an all-year-round commuter service ran between Minehead and Taunton, as well as steam trains for tourists between Minehead and Williton. Western National did not oppose the steam line, but objected to the proposed subsidised commuter service which would have run in competition with its buses.

At a re-convened meeting on 2nd April, the SCC offered the WSR an initial lease for five years, the first 12 months at a peppercorn rent; then £11,400 a year for Minehead to Williton with a peppercorn rent for the remainder. Subsequently the rent would be £14,000, or £4,000 if a commuter service was run - that is a £10,000 subsidy for two years. The minimum commuter service required by the SCC was four each way on Mondays to Fridays and two on Saturdays, the maximum journey time being an hour. The remainder of the £11,400, included £1,400 for preventing coastal erosion.

The SCC rightly considered that the line would be a great tourist attraction in offering its loan of £60,000. The WSR had 160 to 170 volunteers available and anticipated that it could put the Minehead to Williton section in running order in six months, clearing growth on and beside the track and repairing damage caused by vandals and three years of non-use.

A Light Railway Order enabling the line to be worked as a light railway was made on 18th November, 1974 and came into force on 28th November. The SCC then applied to the BRB for the line to be transferred to the SCC and this order was made on 1st September, 1975, coming into effect from 10th September. The 20 years lease and £60,000 loan arrangements were signed on 31st October, 1975. A prospectus was issued on 31st March, 1976 and £65,000 of shares issued to convert the private company into a public company. A total of £95,425 was subscribed and a further issue of 1978 raised £35,000.

The line was re-opened from Minehead to Blue Anchor on 28th March, 1976 by Lord Montague of Beaulieu, Bagnall 0-6-0ST No. 2996 *Victor* being decorated with bunting and a Union Jack. Five thousand passengers were carried in the

Ex-LB&SCR 0-6-0 'Terrier' tank engine No. 32678 and Peckett 0-4-0ST No. 1163 *Whitehead* at Minehead, August 1978. No. 1163, not fitted with vacuum brakes, spent its short life on the WSR as Minehead shed pilot. *Revd Alan Newman*

Bagnall 0-6-0ST No. 2994 *Vulcan* at Minehead, April 1980. Notice the use of a disc instead of a headlamp. *W.H. Harbor/C.G. Maggs Collection*

'4575' class 2-6-2T arrives at Williton with a freight train from Minehead, 11th September, 1987.
Tom Heavyside

'2251' class 0-6-0 No. 3215 ready to depart for Bishop's Lydeard with the 10.15 am on 31st July, 1988. Minehead station has the longest platform of any preserved railway station in the United Kingdom. No. 3215 carries a 'Watchet 1000' celebration headboard. *Hugh Ballantyne*

The exterior of Minehead station on 20th August, 1990. *Author*

first eight days. The line was extended to Williton on 28th August, 1976. That year over 55,000 passengers were carried. The WSR plc was worked with a small full-time staff assisted by WSR volunteers. Between January and August 1976 up to 60 people at a time on the Government's special Temporary Employment Programme helped with the restoration. The line opened to Stogumber on 7th May, 1978 and to Bishop's Lydeard on 9th June, 1979 making its 19¾ miles the longest independent railway in the country.

The two ex-British Leyland Bagnalls, No. 2994 *Vulcan* and No. 2996 *Victor*, from Longbridge Works were powerful, but heavy on coal and water and ex-GWR tank engines were purchased. An 0-6-0 pannier tank, No. 6412, which arrived on 24th March, 1976 in steam from the Torbay Steam Railway, featured in the children's television programme 'The Flockton Flyer' and gave the WSR valuable publicity. Two 2-6-2Ts, Nos. 4561 and 5542, were purchased in 1975 from Woodham's scrapyard at Barry, but needed restoration. (No. 5521 was also purchased at the same time but was subsequently sold.)

By the end of 1980 WSR debts stood at nearly £200,000 and passenger figures had fallen to 70,000. In 1983 passenger figures had risen again, and by 1988 were back at the 1979 level. In 1989 a share issue raised £400,000 to purchase the 99-year lease from the SCC and that same year the WSR carried its millionth passenger. In 1991 a total of 116,573 passengers were carried. WSR ticket sales increased by 52.8 per cent 1987-1992 and ticket sales income 4-fold 1985-92.

The first through train from Taunton to Minehead for 17 years, a special from Manchester, ran on 16th June, 1990, Nos. 4561 and 6412 double-heading the train from Norton Fitzwarren to Minehead and back. As Taunton Cider Company's interchange had to be used, a limit was imposed of six to eight trains using this route annually; the restriction was lifted in 1994. The 24th March, 1991 saw the first through train from Paddington to Minehead for 21 years - the 13-coach Hertfordshire Railtour. BR class '47' No. 47 817 worked the train over the WSR to Bishop's Lydeard where it was taken on to Minehead and back to Norton Fitzwarren by ex-GWR Collett 0-6-0 No. 3205 and ex-Somerset & Dorset Joint Railway class '7F' 2-8-0 No. 53808. On 13th April 'The Flyer' arrived from Hull being brought from Taunton by class '08' diesel shunter No. 08 854, the Taunton station pilot. On 3rd October, 1992 ex-GWR 2-8-0 No. 3822 succeeded in hauling a 19-coach train from Minehead to Bishop's Lydeard and back - almost certainly the longest passenger train to use the branch. On 16th January, 1993 the first Inter-City 125 High Speed Train arrived at Bishop's Lydeard with the 'Quantock Explorer' from Bradford. On 6th June, 1993 the first through train *out* of Minehead was run to York, triple-headed from Bishop's Lydeard by three class '50s'.

The WSR hopes that eventually it will be able to work through to Taunton regularly and Railtrack approves 'in principle' an extension of the WSR to Taunton station, but there are no immediate plans to do so as the capital cost of £740,000 for an independent line from Norton Fitzwarren to Taunton and annual operational costs of £660,000 are high in relation to the anticipated increased revenue accruing from such a scheme.

The WSR has a policy of continuous improvements. In 1991 a new carriage shed was built at Minehead and a visitors' centre opened at Bishop's Lydeard.

On 5th September, 1991 the West Somerset Railway operated a combined ticket with the Paddle Steamer Preservation Society which enabled passengers to travel between Minehead and Watchet using the MV *Balmoral in* one direction and the train in the other direction. *Above*: The 2.00 pm 'Boat Train' is seen leaving Watchet with the MV *Balmoral* in the harbour in the distance. The train worked through to Bishop's Lydeard. *Below*: A view taken later on in the day showing the MV *Balmoral* at Minehead. *(Both) P.G. Barnes*

'45XX' class 2-6-2T No. 4561 arrives at Bishop's Lydeard with a train from Minehead, 31st October, 1991. *Tom Heavyside*

S&DJR '7F' 2-8-0 No. 88 is seen at Williton working the 10.15 am Minehead to Bishop's Lydeard train on 20th July, 1992. *Tom Heavyside*

GWR 4-4-0 No. 3440 *City of Truro* is seen departing from Crowcombe with the 3.55 pm Bishop's Lydeard to Minehead train on 21st July, 1992. *Tom Heavyside*

Beyer, Peacock 'Hymek' B-B diesel-hydraulic type 3 No. D7017 stands at Minehead Platform 1 on 28th October, 1994. *P.G. Barnes*

BR type 1, or class '14' No. 9551 is seen with the 10.40 am goods train from Minehead to Bishop's Lydeard as it approaches the road bridge near Doniford Beach Halt on 29th October, 1994.
P.G. Barnes

Class '08' diesel shunter is coupled to a dmu at Blue Anchor prior to shunting it to the other line where it will form the 1.50 pm to Minehead. *P.G. Barnes*

Taken from the road bridge which carries the A39 over the railway at Williton: English Electric class '50' Co-Co No. 50 149 *Defiance* is seen departing with the 12.10 pm Minehead to Norton Fitzwarren train on 1st October, 1995. Class '42' 'Warship' No. 832 *Onslaught* has just departed for Minehead with the 11.50 am from Norton Fitzwarren and can be seen in the distance.

P.G. Barnes

An Atlas ro-rail shovel enters the pit road at Bishop's Lydeard on 30th July, 1996. This compound is used for the preparation and disposal of engines starting and finishing at Bishop's Lydeard. On the right, old pallets await breaking up for use as firelighters and an ash pile stands to the left of the pit. Gazing into the pit is Dave Bosley, locomotive driver and fitter. The ro-rail shovel can be fitted with a flail head for lineside vegetation clearance. *Author*

The West Somerset Railway Association has a current membership of over 3,000. All its stations are most attractive and worth visiting. Quite apart from their splendid appearance, many stations have some special feature. Re-erected at Williton is the 'Crystal Palace', a steel-framed, former Swindon Works machinery store, now used as a repair shop for locomotives and coaches. The Diesel & Electric Preservation Group established at Williton has secured a grant from the Lottery Heritage Fund to set up a centre there to explain diesel traction and enable restoration activities to be viewed safely. Crowcombe station has a permanent way display; Stogumber has a picnic area; Blue Anchor a GWR museum; Washford a Somerset & Dorset Railway museum and Bishop's Lydeard, a visitors' centre. Several ex-dmu cars are used as very popular open saloons in steam-hauled trains, while a former parcels van has been converted to carry disabled passengers in comfort.

By 1995 the line had been sufficiently upgraded to carry engines with an axle loading of 23½ tons (the axle loading of a 'King' is 22½ tons), while in the winter of 1996 the up platform at Bishop's Lydeard was extended to hold 10 coaches and it is planned to re-signal the station. Locomotive water at Minehead and Bishop's Lydeard comes from the main. When the water authority sought permission for a new water pipe to be laid under the track at Bishop's Lydeard, wayleave was granted on condition that a short branch pipe was laid to the WSR. The timetable requires that one engine be kept overnight at Bishop's Lydeard, so in 1992 a siding, inspection pit and security fencing was installed east of the station. As an odd number of trains is run, this means that an engine starts from the other end of the line on alternate days giving regular travellers a variety of locomotive power. The WSR tries to keep fares at the same level as those of the bus company and passengers prefer to use rail to Doniford as buses travel by an indirect route.

A white board with a black 'X' warns engine drivers of a level crossing and a white light flashes towards the engine when a red signal is displayed to road traffic. To control any lineside fires started by sparks, beaters are carried in each brake compartment.

The WSR is used commercially. In 1996 up to six runs daily were made between Norton Fitzwarren and Bishop's Lydeard by a PCV (Propelling Control Vehicle) train for training main line drivers. A severe storm on 28th October, 1996 broke the sea wall causing Minehead station to be flooded to within three inches of platfrom level and shutting the WSR for four days. Repetition should be prevented by the Minehead Sea Defence Scheme which will need a total of about 150,000 tonnes of stone over five years. On 24th March, 1997 English, Welsh & Scottish-owned English Electric class '37' No. 37 711 hauled the first stone train from Merehead to a siding laid on the site of Butlin's lido at Minehead, for use in the £13.7 million sea defence work. Trains from Merehead Quarry ran on Mondays, Wednesdays and Fridays and from Whatley Quarry on Tuesdays and Thursdays. Through traffic ceased during the height of the holiday season. In the autumn only two or three trains ran weekly. The diesel-electric engine sometimes stalled on the bank between Bishop's Lydeard and Crowcombe, or Kentsford Bank between Watchet and Washford, and on one occasion a steam engine gave assistance from Taunton. The trains carried a WSR

'14XX' class 0-4-2T No. 1450, on loan from the South Devon Railway, outside the former goods shed at Minehead on 10th September, 1996. No. 1450 carries the 82D (Westbury) shed plate.
Author

Class '08' shunter No. 08 850 and class '50' No. 50 117 *Royal Oak* stand outside the diesel depot at Williton on 17th May 1997.
P.G. Barnes

pilotman. Before the departure of Foster-Yeoman Ltd's No. 59 003 *Yeoman Highlander* to Germany in mid-March 1997, German footplate staff had training runs with No. 59 004 *Paul A Hammond* and five wagons on 26th February.

On 16th September, 1997, 21 years after opening, the WSR carried its two millionth passenger, while the 1996 figure of 128,378 passengers was the best ever.

One very caring feature of the WSR is *Lorna Doone*, a disabled persons coach converted from MkI 'BG' van No. M80736. Inside is room for 10-12 wheelchairs secured alongside the windows by floor-mounted locking rails. Each of the two wide doors has a Ratcliff hydraulic lift to raise or lower wheelchairs from, or to, rail level if necessary. At its inauguration on 10th June, 1991 it was the only coach in the EEC fully equiped for disabled passengers.

The coach *Lorna Doone*, converted from a parcels van, is for carrying disabled passengers. In the windows can be seen the reflection of '5101' class 2-6-2T No. 4160 and its leading coach. Notice the WSR garter emblem which owes something to the GWR 'shirt button' roundel. *Author*

The imposing nameboard: 'Taunton for Chard, Minehead, Barnstaple and Ilfracombe Lines', 1st September, 1962. *S.P. Derek*

The down bay platforms at Taunton. '4575' class 2-6-2T No. 5559 with 'B' plate, heads a Barnstaple train on the far left, while sister engine No. 5503 bearing an 'M' plate is ready to work a train to Minehead. Behind '8750' class 0-6-0PT No. 9646 is the corrugated asbestos repair shop. *Lens of Sutton*

Chapter Seven

Description of the Route

When the WSR opened in 1862, Taunton station (163 m. 11 ch. from Paddington), was still of Brunel's one-sided pattern with separate up and down stations. The down platform was lengthened and a new up platform built, both being covered by a train shed, this enlargement complete on 17th August, 1868. In 1895 the station was further extended with bay platforms being added at both ends of the layout to deal with trains terminating from the various branches radiating from Taunton. Congestion returned and the track from Cogload Junction through Taunton station to Norton Fitzwarren was quadrupled in the early 1930s, the re-modelled Taunton station being completed on 20th December, 1931. The whistle code for a train ready to leave the Minehead departure bay at Taunton was 2-3, while Minehead branch trains gave three long whistles (Barnstaple branch two) at West Junction box, Taunton, and also carried a white disc bearing a black 'M', Barnstaple branch trains carrying a 'B'.

As an economy measure, Norton Fitzwarren signal box closed on 1st March, 1970 and west of Silk Mill Crossing signal box the former up relief line became the Minehead single line. From 27th February, 1983 until December 1992 this connection was used as a private siding for Taunton Cider Company's traffic.

Norton Fitzwarren (165 m. 8 ch.), was originally a 2-road station built in 1873 by Messrs Phillips of Bristol following the opening of the Devon & Somerset Railway on 8th June, 1871 to Wiveliscombe. A stone station building stood on the up platform and a timber waiting shelter on the down. When the track was quadrupled on the up side, the original platforms were replaced by two islands on 2nd December, 1931, the office block of the new station being on the up side at ground level. Crossovers permitted a Minehead train to use any platform. Until July 1931 when Taunton became a 'closed' station, stopping trains were allowed two to three minutes at Norton Fitzwarren for ticket examination and collection. Norton Fitzwarren closed to passengers on 30th October, 1961.

Norton Fitzwarren signal box erected in 1931 had a 131-lever frame. Its signalmen, as well as controlling signals and points for the main line and branches, had to take or fetch the electric token for the Minehead branch and the electric staff for the Barnstaple line. While out of his box doing this, he could not answer the bells, thus delaying trains. The situation was improved by doubling the branches as far as the first station; that to Bishop's Lydeard on 8th June, 1936 and to Milverton on 21st February, 1937. Until this latter date, at the junction west of Norton Fitzwarren station, the Barnstaple branch left the Minehead branch immediately it curved from the main line, but from 21st February, 1937 the Barnstaple branch had its own connection with the main line and was independent of the Minehead branch. Norton Siding, ½ mile west of Norton Fitzwarren Junction towards Bishop's Lydeard on the up side, was lifted by 1890.

Bishop's Lydeard (168 m. 21 ch.), like all the WSR stations, originally had only a single platform on the down side, but to ease working an up platform,

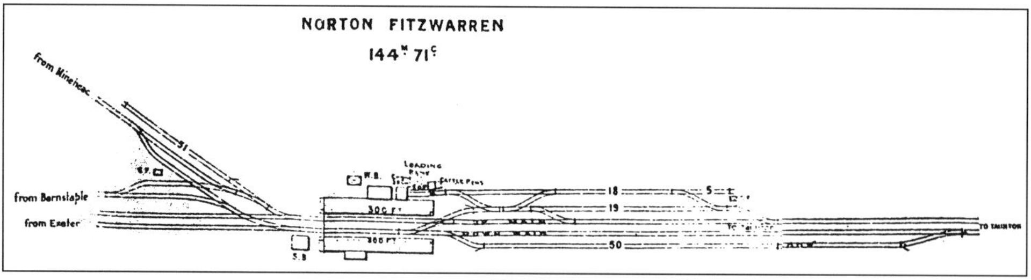

View down at Norton Fitzwarren *c.* 1905. Notice the typical B&ER overhanging eaves of the station building on the up platform. Beyond the footbridge is the junction for lines to Barnstaple and Minehead, the latter curving off the Barnstaple branch. The goods yard hand crane is prominent on the right. *Author's Collection*

An up broad gauge express passes Norton Junction signal box c. 1890. The Minehead branch curves round to the right, while the Barnstaple branch curves left from the Minehead line immediately beyond the junction and to the left of the ground frame cabin. *Author's Collection*

The view west from the footbridge of Norton Fitzwarren station *c.* 1925. *Author's Collection*

Norton Fitzwarren down, 29th October, 1990, with cider vans standing on what was the Minehead branch. The house on the far right used to be the Railway Hotel. *Author*

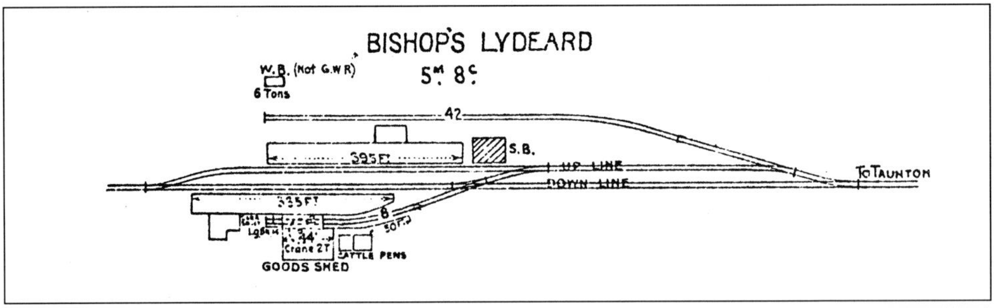

A view of Bishop's Lydeard station looking towards Norton Fitzwarren on 2nd July, 1934.
Brunel University: Mowat/Locomotive Collection

Bishop's Lydeard, showing the main building on the down platform, 28th August, 1967.
Derrick Payne

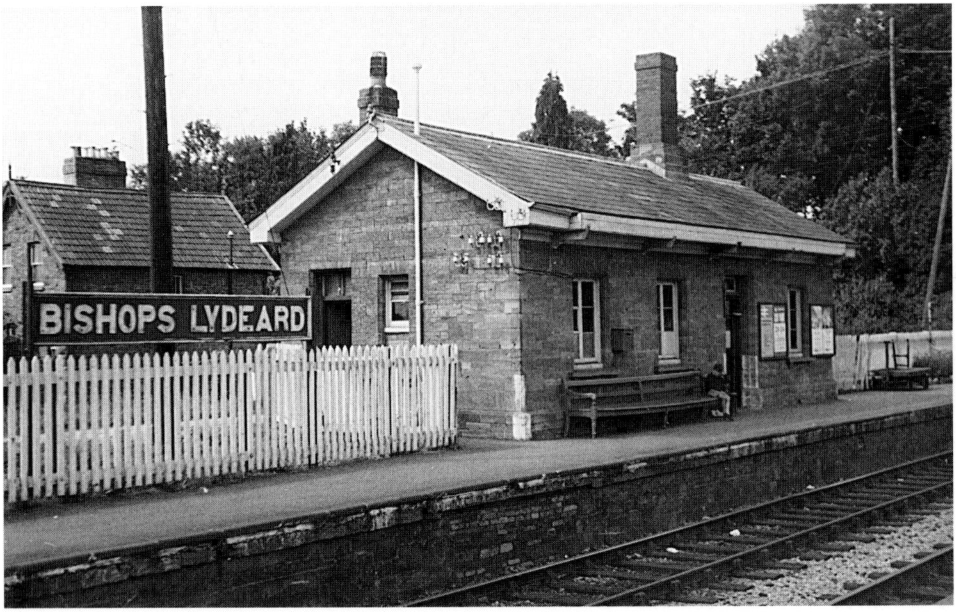

Bishop's Lydeard, view in the down direction. On the right the gradient post on bridge rail, marks a change from 1 in 356 to 1 in 1,547, 28th August, 1967. *Derrick Payne*

'Hymek' diesel-hydraulic No. D7017 (now preserved on the WSR) enters Bishop's Lydeard with the 10.00 am Taunton to Minehead, 8th June, 1963. *Author*

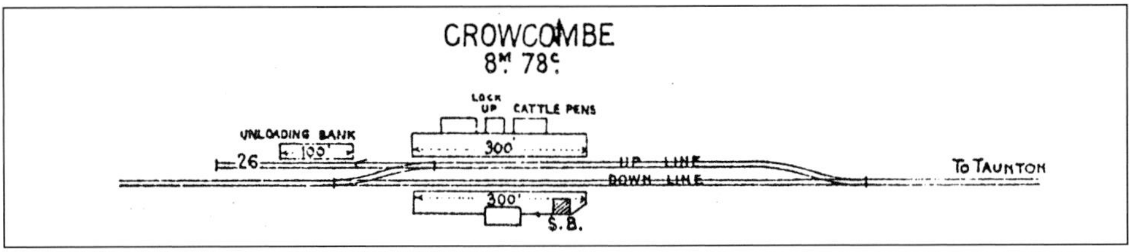

Bridge rails on longitudinal sleepers were still in place when this view of Crowcombe station was taken *c.* 1900 looking towards Norton Fitzwarren. As an economy measure, the building had no canopy. *Author's Collection*

Crowcombe: down direction on 25th August, 1965 showing the goods siding and loading bank beyond the passenger station. Notice the four fire buckets placed outside the building. *Derrick Payne*

1,000 ft-long passing loop and signal box opened on 2nd July, 1906. In 1943 a Ministry of Works siding was added to the goods yard. A food reserve arrived by rail for the adjacent Government buffer depot, being distributed to the Taunton area by road. As the gradient at the station fell at 1 in 85 towards Norton Fitzwarren, rules stipulated that before a goods engine was uncoupled from its train, the brake in the guard's van had to be securely applied and sufficient wagon brakes and sprags used to prevent the train moving. Six sprags, each ten yds apart, were required to be kept between the main lines.

Crowcombe (172 m. 11 ch.), was called Crowcombe Heathfield until 1st December, 1889, and reverted to its original name once more in 1992, had a single platform with a small, low stone building until 1879 when another platform was built on the down side. The loop and platforms were lengthened on 22nd April, 1934 and the signal box closed on 5th March, 1967. The station served scattered dwellings rather than a village and was also used by groups, or even train loads of walkers bound for the Quantock Hills. Crowcombe is situated at the summit of the line and because of this, special instructions were issued regarding shunting. It was forbidden to detach vehicles on the main line, this operation having to be carried out in the up loop, the station's solitary siding leading off from this. Sprags had to be kept between the loop lines and to the rear of the up home signal. An overhead cable way brought stone from Triscombe Quarry's crushing plant to this GWR siding. The station lacked a goods shed. The loop was reinstated in May 1994, the upper floor of the new signal box coming from Ebbw Vale Sidings South and the frame from Frome North box.

The station master lived in a house 200 yds north of the station towards the overbridge. It was one of the daily jobs of the lad porter to hand pump water to this house from the station well. The task took over an hour and a full tank was indicated by an overflow from the pipe beside the station chimney.

Leigh Wood level crossing (173 m. 48 ch.), was where in 1913 worked one of the very few women employed in traffic operations on a British railway at that time. When employed by the GWR at Chard, Mrs Hill's husband met with a serious accident in 1880. He was transferred to the relatively light job at Leigh Wood Crossing, but was never again fit for duty. His wife undertook his work operating the gates and carried it out so efficiently that, after his death in 1881, she was allowed to remain in charge.

Leigh Bridge (174 m. 6 ch.) was a 750 ft long crossing loop opened on 16th July, 1933 to split the six mile-long single line section to speed the service on peak summer Saturdays. The box closed on 8th May, 1964.

Stogumber (174 m. 66 ch.), because of its position on an embankment, had its single platform and waiting shelter separate from the ground level station building on the opposite side of the track. In the early 1900s the platform was lengthened towards Taunton using old sleepers and in 1933 extended towards Watchet using concrete supports for a surface of old sleepers. The signal box, not a block post, closed on 6th April, 1926, being replaced by two ground frames. The siting of the goods shed opposite the centre of the passenger platform was rather unusual, though copied at Washford, Dunster and Minehead. In summer the siding was occupied by a camping coach whose

A 'Hymek' enters Crowcombe with a down train, 25th August, 1965. *Derrick Payne*

At Crowcombe the 8.50 am Saturdays-only Paddington to Minehead on 18th July, 1970, was worked by Swindon Inter-City dmu comprising what appears to be three units totalling 12 cars. Unit No. 509 is leading when seen here with the return working, the 1.00 pm Minehead to Paddington. The down platform has fallen into disuse. *Hugh Ballantyne*

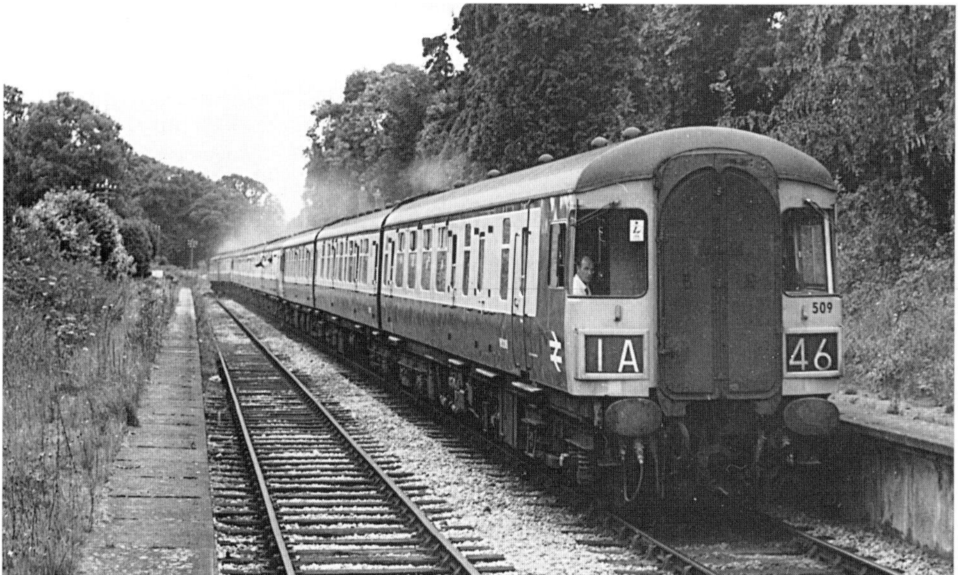

Leigh Bridge crossing loop and signal box on 2nd July, 1934. It had been opened in July of the previous year. *Brunel University: Mowat/Locomotive Collection*

Stogumber, view down *c.* 1883. Notice the signal box, (closed 6th April, 1926), the waiting shelter, the longitudinal sleepers, goods shed and loading gauge. The goods shed obscures the view of an up train from the foot crossing. *Author's Collection*

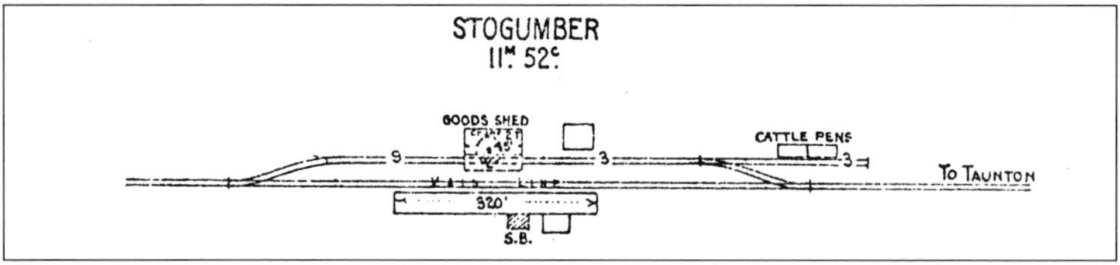

Stogumber, view up. Notice the sleeper-built platform, access to which is across the main track. Near the stone station building is a milk tank wagon containing the water supply for the camping coach stabled on the cattle dock siding. Notice the Leigh Bridge distant signal beyond the platform. *Lens of Sutton*

The 4.45 pm Taunton to Minehead leaves Stogumber station on 30th June, 1967. On the far right is the disused station office block and centre right is the rubble left following the demolition of the goods shed two years earlier. *Author*

occupants obtained their water from a 6-wheel ex-milk tanker. As the station was on an incline of 1 in 91 falling towards Williton, six sprags were required to be kept 10 yds apart by the side of the line between the ground frames.

The falling gradient continued to Williton (178 m. 7 ch.), up trains facing a start on a rising gradient of 1 in 99. The station had but a single platform until about 1871 when the up platform and loop were put in. The signal box is the only one of the B&ER design still in existence and furthermore is in working order. The level crossing at the up end of the station was paralleled by an overbridge in 1873. Carrying the main road, it was reconstructed in pre-stressed concrete in 1952. The cattle pen siding, taken out of use on 19th May, 1965, was reinstated on 17th January, 1968 for engineer's use. Watering facilities were provided at the station, the Outdoor Department of Taunton shed maintaining the pump. Until the opening of the Minehead Railway, Williton was the transfer point for passengers proceeding westwards by road coach.

The station was prone to flooding. This happened in November 1875 and on 24th October, 1882 water was 2 ft deep and the first two trains got through, but the 11.30 am ex-Taunton and the 11.45 am ex-Minehead which crossed at 12.15 encountered problems. The down train failed to draw into the station, water having displaced the rails. Passengers and luggage were transferred from one to the other by means of a trolley, the trains leaving 2½ hours late.

Doniford Beach Halt (178 m. 78 ch.), opened on 27th June, 1987 by the preserved WSR was built from concrete components from Montacute, on the closed Taunton to Yeovil line. It soon closed because of access problems, but re-opened on 14th July, 1992. On 31st March a cliff fall beyond the halt dropped the boundary fence to the beach, but West Somerset District Council restored the sea defences at a cost of approximately £140,000.

The office block at Watchet (179 m. 62 ch.), is odd in as much as it was placed at right angles to the platform, originating from the fact that initially the station formed the line's terminus. It is also curious that, although a principal station on the branch, it has only ever had one platform; this was lengthened in 1934. The tall signal box on the embankment behind the passenger platform closed on 11th August, 1926 and was replaced by two ground frames controlling entry and exit of the goods and harbour lines. Access to the Eastern Pier was via a wagon turntable. A 40 ton weighbridge was situated on the loop line between the up end of the platform and the harbour. As engines were forbidden to pass over the weighbridge, the track was gauntletted. East of the station is Govier's Lane foot crossing and to protect its users, the GWR installed a warning bell. As the track circuit provided to operate it was 622 yds distant for up trains and 1,023 yds for down trains, a shunting movement would not cause it to ring. In such circumstances the station master was required to provide a porter to protect the crossing. In the summer of 1938 Watchet was still using B&ER 'To Falmouth' luggage labels.

A ¼ mile beyond the station was Watchet Paper Mills, the facing private sidings in use from 31st January, 1929 until 2nd February, 1965. As they were on a falling gradient of 1 in 40, the guard and shunter had to apply sufficient brakes and sprags on the leading vehicles to control them. Six sprags had to be left 10 yds apart on the main line and six on the loop siding. It was forbidden

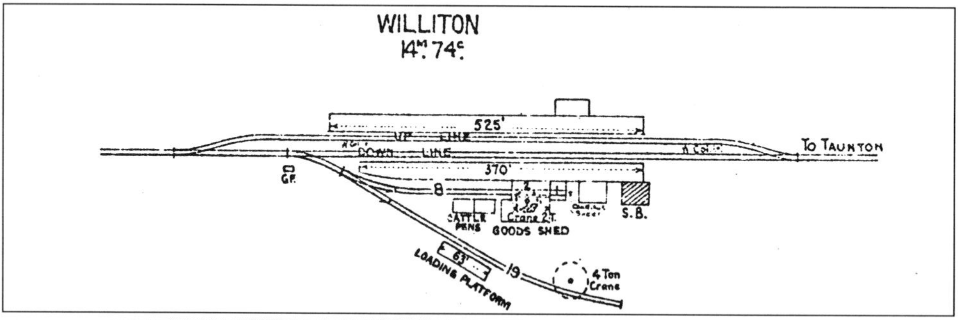

Two views of Williton signal box and level crossing which is at the Taunton end of the station on the down side. *Above;* in September 1959. *Below;* in August 1967.

D.J. Powell and Derrick Payne

Bridge rails on longitudinal sleepers can be clearly seen in this view of Williton station taken around the turn of the century. *Lens of Sutton*

'Hymek' diesel-hydraulic No. D7017 at Williton with the 11.15 am Minehead to Paddington train, 17th August, 1963. This locomotive was only just over a year old at the time. *R.E. Toop*

Williton station showing the shelter on the up platform and the footbridge on 18th September, 1959.
D.J. Powell

View south from the footbridge towards the overbridge renewed in pre-stressed concrete in 1952, the parallel level crossing showing at the foot of the picture. To the right is the pump house with water tank above which the station's water cranes. Between it and the overbridge is the span over the Doniford Stream. The up line shows trap points to prevent a train entering the single line against the signal at danger, and catch points to divert a backwards runaway, 28th August, 1967.
Derrick Payne

BR type 4 1 Co-Co 1 class '45' D120 passes Doniford Beach Halt with the 10.45 am Bishop's Lydeard to Minehead train, 1st October, 1995. *P.G. Barnes*

BR type 2 Bo-Bo class '25' No. 7523 is seen passing Doniford Beach Halt with the 2.48 pm Williton to Minehead goods train on 16th May, 1997. The platform now boasts a pagoda building. *P.G. Barnes*

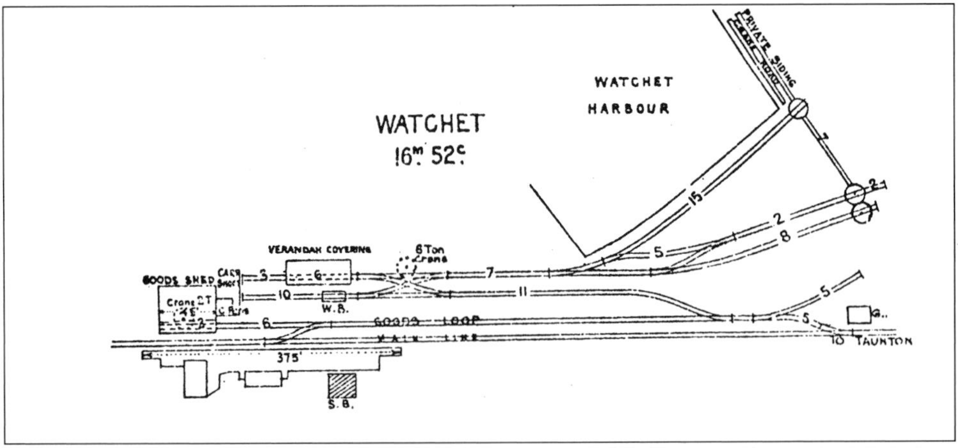

A standard gauge 0-6-0ST at Watchet *c.* 1900. Notice the tall signal box left of the goods shed; lengths of rail stored in the foreground and the outside-framed body of the brake van.

Author's Collection

Watchet, 21st July, 1957. The distant signal is for Kentsford. Watchet West ground frame is at the foot of the telegraph post. *N.C. Simmons*

Watchet on 31st July, 1953 showing the goods shed, weighbridge and track used by vehicles not being weighed. The post of the loading gauge can be seen, right, for gauging wagons on the line leading from the Harbour. *Author*

Watchet station buildings on 11th September, 1987. *P.G. Barnes*

A pannier tank heads a goods train to Minehead as it crosses the trackbed of the West Somerset Mineral Railway just west of Watchet in 1962. *S.A. Leleux*

to loose-shunt wagons down into these sidings, or uncouple them until the engine had been brought to a stand at the Stop Board. Subsequent movements of the wagons were carried out by the paper company's horses, at least until 1947, but at some subsequent date by a Fordson tractor. It was permitted to propel up to 15 wagons between Watchet and the paper mill sidings, and returning to Watchet, wagons could be drawn without a brake van at the rear provided that the guard or shunter rode or walked alongside the last vehicle, which was required to display a tail lamp. Ingoing traffic was coal, waste paper and dyes, while 6 to 14 van loads of paper left daily.

Beyond, the Minehead Railway crossed the West Somerset Mineral Railway at an angle of 30 degrees by a girder bridge. Here the WSMR is now a footpath. Further on where the two lines were at the same level, on at least five occasions a temporary connection was put in. The first was on Sunday 8th January, 1899 when, following the closure of the WSMR, a long train consisting of three GWR engines, the WSMR 0-6-0ST *Pontypool*, three coaches and 50 wagons were taken to Watchet. Next morning they worked via Swindon and Gloucester, through to Ebbw Vale, where the WSMR's owners had their headquarters. The connection was put in again on Sunday 30th June, 1907 to transfer ex-Metropolitan Railway 4-4-0T No. 37 for the re-opening of the WSMR and on 28th June, 1910 for its removal, together with wagons. The fourth occasion was on 17th December, 1911 when two ex-West Midland Railway 2-4-0 tender engines, GWR Nos. 212 and 213, were transferred to WSMR track for demonstrating the Angus system of automatic train control. They were transferred back to the GWR on 4th November, 1917 and stored at the rear of Taunton shed until about 1919.

Kentsford Loop (180 m. 42 ch.), opened 10th July, 1933 until 7th May, 1964, was only switched in for summer services.

Washford (182 m. 11 ch.), at the head of the line's secondary summit, had a signal box on its single platform. This box closed on 24th August, 1952, though it had only contained levers since 11th August, 1926 when its instruments were transferred to the booking office. Following closure of the box, sidings were worked by a ground frame. A cattle market was adjacent to the station. Washford is now the headquarters of the Somerset & Dorset Railway Trust. Beyond, the line descends the steepest gradient on the branch, 1 in 65 for just over a mile through a principal cutting ¾ mile in length reaching a maximum depth of nearly 40 ft. Beyond is an embankment ¾ mile in length and up to 30 ft high.

Blue Anchor (184 m. 32 ch.), named after a public house, was unique on the branch in having its original platform on the up, and not the down, side in order to give direct access to the beach. Of simple design, Blue Anchor Excursion Platform as it was originally called, was not open all year round. A loop and down platform were added on 5th January, 1904. No goods siding was provided until 1st April, 1913. As the station was on a gradient of 1 in 91 falling towards Dunster, before an engine was detached from a goods train the guard's brake had to be securely applied and sufficient wagon brakes and sprags used to secure it from running away.

Latterly this goods siding was used by camping coaches. The GWR introduced camping coaches at Easter 1934, one of the first being at Blue Anchor. By 1957 the

A view from the trackbed of the West Somerset Mineral Railway between Washford and Watchet, the Minehead branch is on the left, 13th August, 1962. *S.A. Leleux*

A 'Metro' class 2-4-0T is seen at Washford in the 1920s with a train for Minehead. *Lens of Sutton*

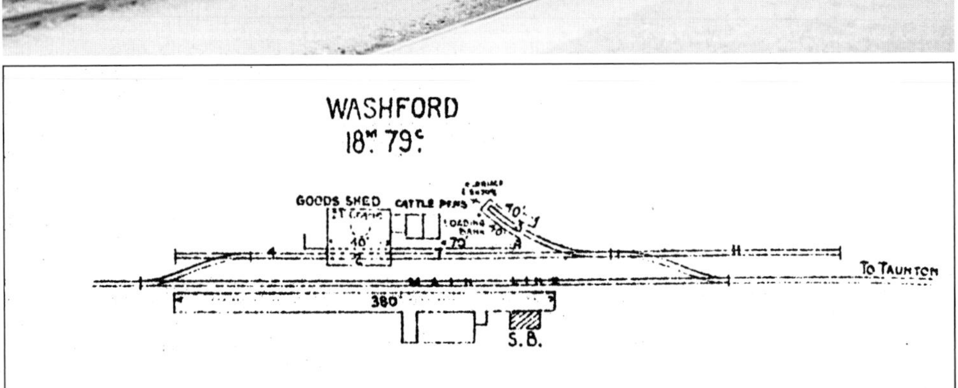

Washford *c.* 1910. Notice the low signals; the small signal box; the wicker cage outside for transporting small animals. Beyond the station building is an attractive display of shrubs and small flower beds while between the photographer and the cattle dock is an oil engine.

Lens of Sutton

Washford on 13th August, 1993. *Author*

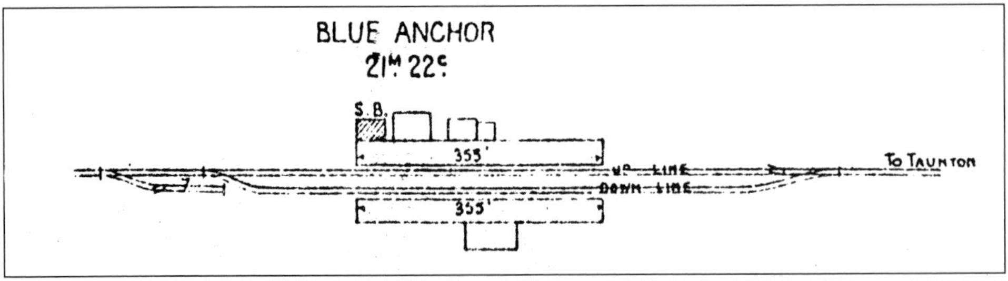

Blue Anchor view looking towards Minehead *c.* 1920. The down platform was added in 1904. The truncated appearance of the nearest building on the up platform, the Ladies' Room, is due to its close proximity to the boundary fence. Notice the attractive flower bed.

Author's Collection

A view of the buildings on the up platform at Blue Anchor in August 1966. *D.J. Powell*

An unrecorded 'Hymek' diesel-hydraulic arrives at Blue Anchor with an up train. In this 1967 view, shrubs are beginning to encroach on the platform. *Derrick Payne*

Park Royal 2-car dmu consisting of driving trailer composite No. 56168 and motor brake second No. 50413 at Blue Anchor with the 9.45 am Stogumber to Minehead, 1st June, 1978. The old waiting shelter between the office block and the Ladies' Room has been demolished, but not yet replaced. *Author*

Both sides of the counter at Blue Anchor's booking office, 20th August, 1962.
(Both) S.A. Leleux

'4575' class 2-6-2T No. 5563 arrives at Blue Anchor with a train from Minehead, 20th August, 1962. *S.A. Leleux*

'61XX' class 2-6-2T No. 6146 approaches Blue Anchor with a train from Minehead, 21st August, 1962. In the foreground can be seen the ground signal for the siding, which at that time housed camping coaches. *S.A. Leleux*

Plan of GWR camping coach, Blue Anchor, 1936.

CAMPING COACH EQUIPMENT—Six Persons

CUTLERY.
6 Large Knives.
6 Small Knives.
6 Large Forks.
6 Small Forks.
6 Dessert Spoons.
6 Tea Spoons.
4 Table Spoons.
Bread Knife.
Carving Knife and Fork.
Tin Opener.
Cork Screw.

CROCKERY.
6 Dinner Plates.
6 Pudding Plates.
6 Tea Plates.
6 Soup Plates.
2 Veg. Tureens.
2 Dishes.
6 Cups.
6 Saucers.
6 Tumblers.
1 Cruet.
2 Jugs.
2 Pudding Basins.
1 Tea Pot.
1 Sugar Bowl.
6 Egg Cups.

BEDCLOTHES.
6 Under Blankets.
12 Sheets.
18 Rugs.
6 Pillows.
6 Pillow Cases.
6 Pillow Slips.

KITCHEN UTENSILS.
2 Enamel Saucepans and Steamer.
1 Frying Pan.
1 Kettle (6 pints).
1 Pan Scrub.
1 Enamel Bowl.
1 Enamel Jug.
2 Enamel Water Buckets.
1 Enamel Sanitary Bucket.
1 Enamel Refuse Bucket.
1 Broom.
1 Dripping Tin.
1 Colander.
1 Handbrush.
1 Bread Board.
1 Scrubbing Brush.

MISCELLANEOUS.
3 Oil Lamps for Bedrooms.
1 Duplex Lamp for Sitting Room.
1 Hurricane Lamp.
1 Jug for Paraffin.
4 Chambers.
1 Dustbin.
1 Funnel.
3 Deck Chairs.
6 Chairs.
1 Enamelled Sink.
1 Small Kitchen Table with Drawers.
1 Primus Stove with Oven.
1 Mirror.

OTHER LINEN.
2 Table Cloths.
1 Dish Cloth.
3 Tea Cloths.
3 Dusters.
6 Towels.
2 Roller Towels.
1 Oven Cloth.

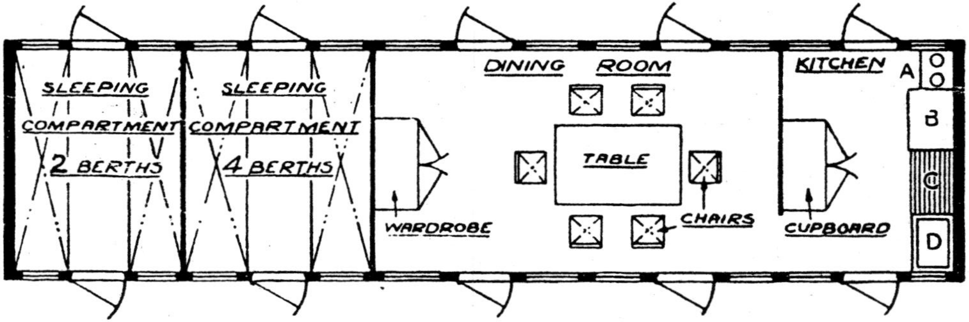

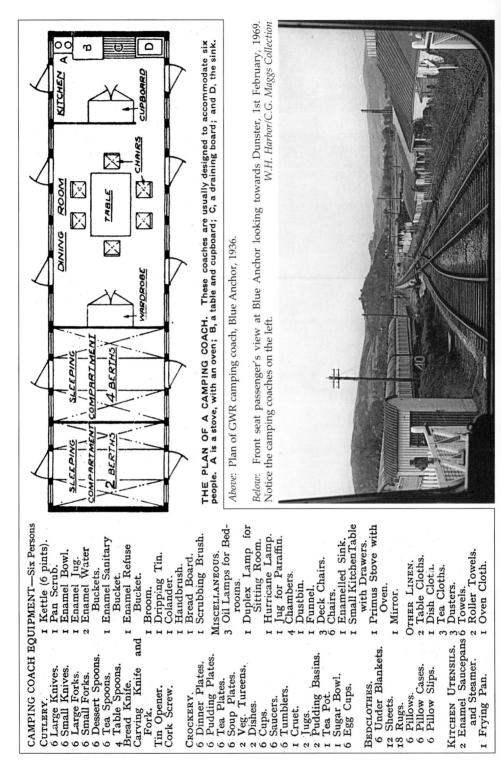

THE PLAN OF A CAMPING COACH. These coaches are usually designed to accommodate six people. A is a stove, with an oven; B, a table and cupboard; C, a draining board; and D, the sink.

Above: Plan of GWR camping coach, Blue Anchor, 1936.

Below: Front seat passenger's view at Blue Anchor looking towards Dunster, 1st February, 1969. Notice the camping coaches on the left. *W.H. Harbor/C.G. Maggs Collection*

two 8-berth camping coaches had a weekly rental varying from £7 in the low season to £11 10s. in the high season. Latterly, the camping coaches at Blue Anchor were owned by the Railway Staff Association for members' holidays.

The line crosses Ker Moor slightly inland from the coast to Dunster (186 m. 24 ch.). The single platform station has quite an imposing entrance due to the fact that it was the station for the Luttrell family of Dunster Castle, promoters of the railway. Heads of State and Indian princes passed through the station doorway, while polo ponies and their grooms arrived in special trains in horse boxes. Whenever it was necessary to detach a vehicle from a down passenger train, the vehicle to be uncoupled had to stand short of the points. After it was detached, the train was required to draw ahead to the platform and the vehicle pushed into the siding by hand before the train's departure. Vehicles detached from an up passenger train had to be placed in the siding before being uncoupled. Six sprags were required to be kept by the side of the line, 10 yds apart.

The track layout at Dunster was a replica of Washford. The signal box on the platform closed on 4th August, 1926 and was replaced by two ground frames. On 19th March, 1934 a second-hand signal box from South Wales was opened at the west end of the station to control the adjacent level crossing and the commencement of the (now) double track to Minehead. In order that Minehead signal box could be closed, on 27th March, 1966 the former up and down tracks between Dunster and Minehead became two single lines: the down serving Minehead bay platform, and the former up line giving access to the main platform. Although normally only the main platform was used at Minehead, the bay was essential to accommodate the extra summer traffic. The down advanced starting signal at Dunster carried the fixed distant for Minehead, while Minehead's up advanced starter had Dunster's fixed distant. Today Dunster level crossing is ungated with no bell or lights. A 5 mph restriction is imposed and the whistle required to be sounded, but at Sea Lane level crossing east of the station where speeds are higher, there is a bell and flashing lights.

In connection with the full reinstatement of the redeveloped Minehead station layout, on 20th November, 1977 the complete Dunster signal box structure was jacked up, slid onto a specially made truck and moved by rail to Minehead - an event surely unique in railway operations.

Between Dunster and Minehead the line runs at an average of 4 ft above the general level of the land, and a trench was cut either side of the embankment to drain the marshy ground. On 13th November, 1875 Mr Hole, station master at Dunster, discovered that floods had displaced ballast and rails. A train stopped each side of the break and passengers had to wade through the floods. Men repaired the damage on Sunday the 14th and traffic resumed on the Monday.

The original layout at Minehead, (187 m. 76 ch.), was small and rather cramped, with a single platform, (sometimes occupied by two trains at a time); goods shed road; cattle dock road; run-round loop; engine shed and turntable. The original signal box closed in 1905 to permit the platform to be lengthened and another face used. This work was completed by 1st July, 1905. Colonel Yorke carried out a Board of Trade inspection of improvements at Minehead on 22nd July, 1905 and reported:

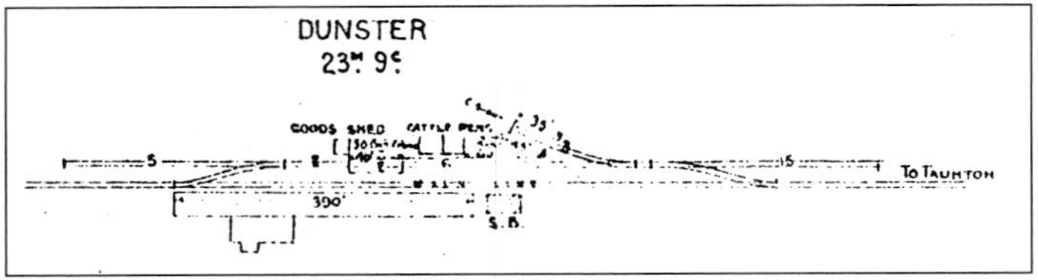

Dunster station and goods shed, view looking towards Minehead. The cattle dock is in the extreme right of the picture. A box van stands just outside the goods shed. The gradient post on the right marks a change from 1 in 223 to 1 in 1,320

Brunel University: Mowat/Locomotive Collection

'Hymek' diesel-hydraulic No. D7041 with the 3.10 pm Minehead to Paddington train comes off the double track on to the single line at Dunster station, 17th August, 1963. The Raleigh bicycle with front dyno-hub very likely belongs to the signalman. *R.E. Toop*

Dunster goods shed, 13th August, 1993. *Author*

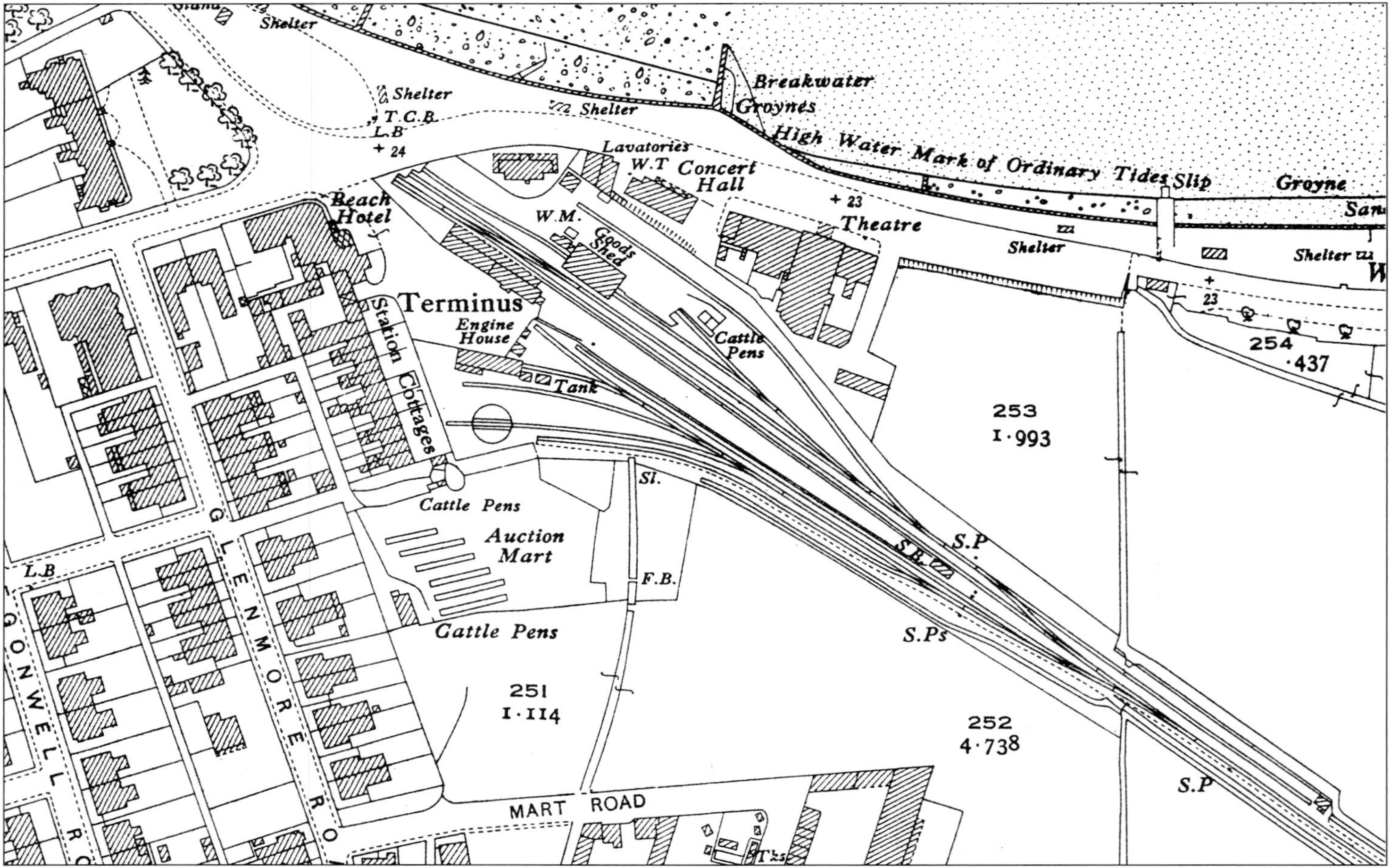

Minehead station.

Reproduced from the 25", 1929 Ordnance Suvey Map

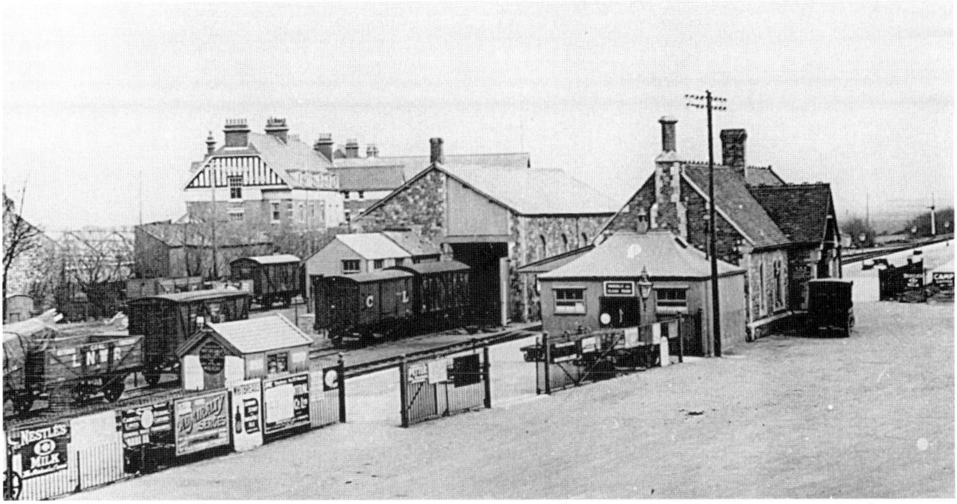

Minehead on 15th June, 1923. Rolling stock belongs to the London & North Western Railway, Midland Railway, Cheshire Lines Committee and Cannock & Rugeley Colliery. Enamel signs advertise Nestlé's milk, Pullar's of Perth dry cleaning, house furnishing, Admiralty serges, Whitbread's ale and stout, Petter's oil engines, Cerebos salt, State Express cigarettes, Robertson's marmalade, Palethorpe's sausages and Camp coffee. *GWR*

Horse-drawn vehicles lined up outside Minehead station for onwards conveyance of passengers to hotels and villages. Next to the cast-iron pagoda labelled 'Parcels and Cloak Room' stands the Lynton coach, drawn by four horses. *Author's Collection*

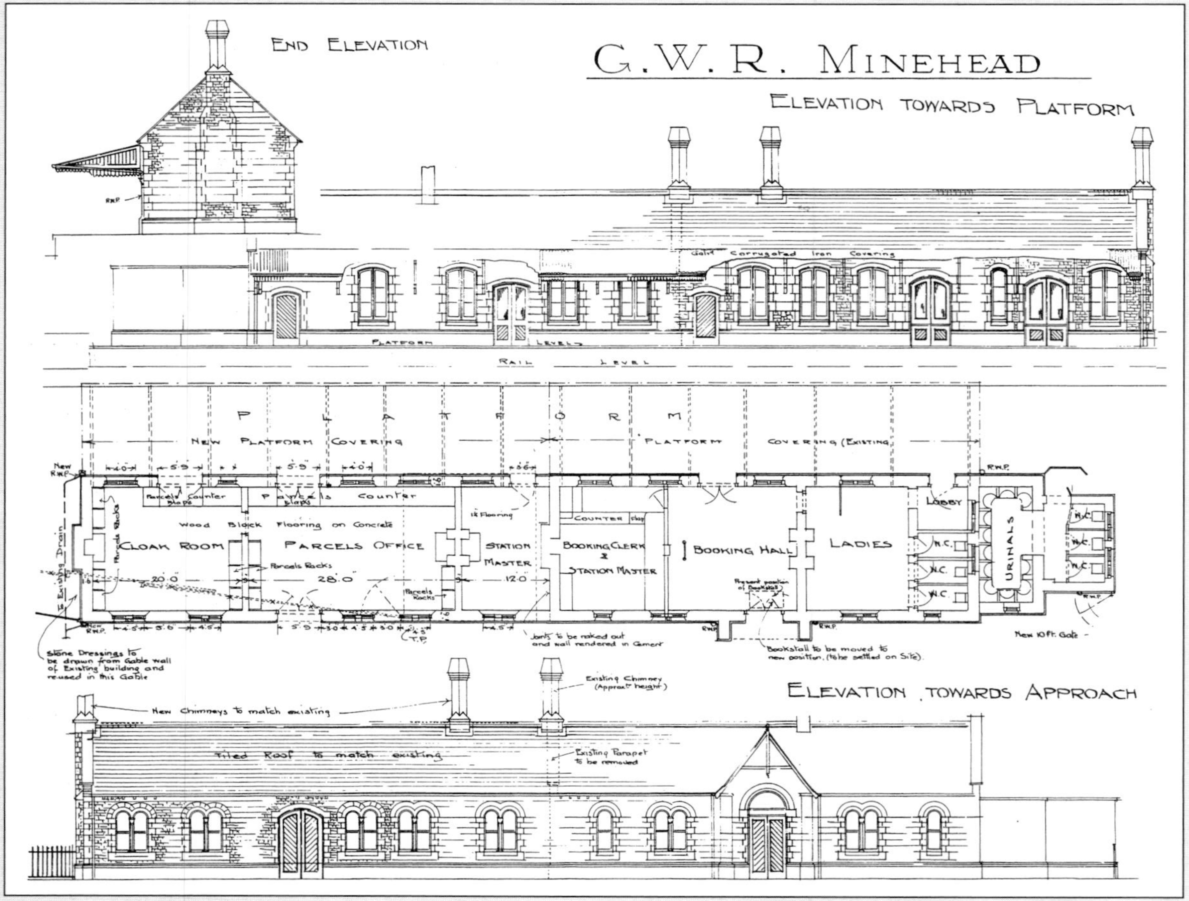

Drawing of the GWR passenger station at Minehead.

GWR

The throat of Minehead station looking towards Dunster on 18th September, 1959. The signal box that was opened at the time of signalling improvements on the branch in 1934 can be seen in the distance beyond the water tank. *D.J. Powell*

'4575' class 2-6-2T No. 5542 of 83B (Taunton) shed arrives at Minehead on 24th August, 1950. *Revd Alan Newman*

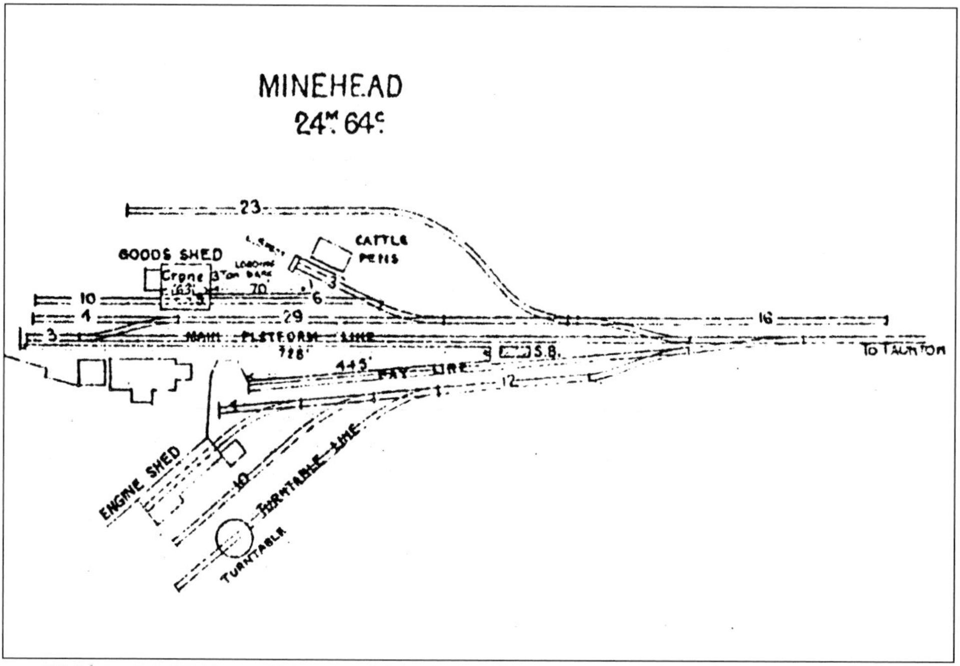

'43XX' class 2-6-0 No. 6323 at Minehead *c.* 1958. *M.E.J. Deane*

The wide platform at Minehead capable of dealing with crowds. '5101' class 2-6-2T No. 4157 is leaving with a 4-coach train to Taunton, 21st July, 1957. *N.C. Simmons*

''2251' class 0-6-0 No. 2213 stands at Minehead awaiting departure to Taunton with a passenger train. The engine shed can be seen on the extreme left of the picture, with the cattle dock just visible on the extreme right. *Lens of Sutton*

'43XX' class 2-6-0 No. 6323 carrying express headlamps, has been uncoupled from its 5-coach train and is about to take the loop before proceeding to the engine shed, 21st July, 1957.
N.C. Simmons

A Swindon Works 3-car cross-country dmu stands at Minehead station's main platform on 1st February, 1968. The buffer stops are almost entirely rail-built. The former goods shed is to the left.
W.H. Harbor/Author's Collection

These comprise the extension of the existing platform, the provision of a new platform line for passenger traffic, alterations in the siding connections, the construction of a new signal box and the re-signalling of the whole place.

The signal box contains 19 levers in use and six spare levers.

The interlocking being correct and the arrangements satisfactory, I can now recommend the Board of Trade to sanction the use of the new works at this place.

Two long mileage sidings were brought into to use on 23rd July, 1931. The 1905 signal box was replaced on 15th January, 1934 by one from Pensnett North on the Wolverhampton-Stourbridge Jn line, when the platform was further lengthened to allow it to take a 16-coach train, and a canopy about 350 ft in length erected. A run-round loop was put in for the bay platform and a carriage siding laid parallel with it. Both running-round roads had points at the buffer stops worked by adjacent single levers, electrically locked. Near the gate at the west end of the platform was a booking office for the Lynton coach which was horse-drawn until 1919, this form of traction remaining until then, partly as a tourist attraction. During World War I a mule transit camp was established at Middlecombe and animals were taken on to the war fronts by rail. If possible locomotives tried to avoid taking water at Minehead because it came from a mains supply and had to be paid for, whereas water at Williton belonged to the railway.

In 1934 Mrs G.F. Luttrell of Dunster Castle and wife of the GWR Director, offered a prize of £5, rather more than most railwaymen's pay for a week, to the station on the branch making the greatest progress in garden cultivation. Minehead won it for the 1934-35 season.

The bay platform and loading dock, Minehead, 1st February, 1968.

W.H. Harbor/Author's Collection

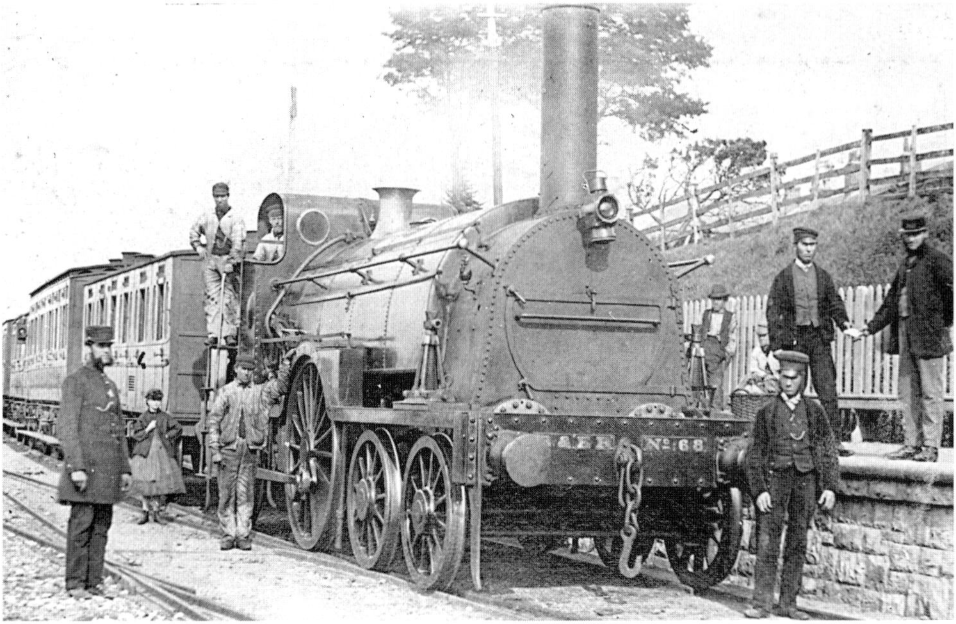

B&ER 4-4-0ST No. 68 at Watchet *c.* 1867. Built in 1867 it became GWR No. 2041 and was withdrawn in 1880. Notice the jacks beside the smokebox and the lack of vacuum brake. The coaches are of various heights and widths. *Courtesy: H.H. Hole*

A view onto the footplate of a Collett '2251' class 0-6-0 on an up goods at Watchet. *Author's Collection*

Chapter Eight

Locomotives and Locomotive Sheds

The Bristol & Exeter Railway ran broad gauge 4-4-0STs such as Nos. 51, 61, 68 and 74 on the line. When the branch was converted to standard gauge the GWR used engines of the 0-6-0ST, and 2-4-0T classes, while in the 1920s '44XX' and '45XX' 2-6-2Ts were used, the '45XX' class superseding 'Metro' class 2-4-0Ts in 1927. In the 1930s traffic was worked by 'Dean Goods' and '2251' class 0-6-0s; '43XX' class 2-6-0s; 'Bulldog' 4-4-0s; large and small 2-6-2Ts, though '3150' class 2-6-2Ts, which were 'Red' engines, were not allowed on the branch because of their weight. By the mid-1950s passenger trains tended to be worked by '57XX' class 0-6-0PTs, the '2251' class being responsible for freight duties. In October 1961 BR Standard class '3' 2-6-2Ts began sharing duties with '41XX' and '51XX' 2-6-2Ts which had substantially replaced '45XX' engines of the same wheel arrangement on the branch. With dieselisation, diesel-hydraulic North British 'D63XX' class and 'Hymeks' appeared on locomotive-hauled trains. Dmus were Derby Works 3-car Suburban, the Gloucester Railway, Carriage & Wagon Co. Cross-Country, with Swindon Cross-Country units. The 8.50 am Paddington to Minehead, and its return 1.00 pm Minehead to Paddington, was a Swindon Inter City unit.

Tank engines with automatic token changing apparatus were:

'4575' fitted July 1933	4581, 5503/5/21/37/42/3/51/71
'4575' fitted June/July 1934	5501/2/4/22/5/69
In BR days '5101' class 2-6-2Ts	4117 and 5172

Tender engines with automatic token changing apparatus included:

'43XX' class 2-6-0s	4339/49/61, 6305/23/54/63/4/72/83/98, 7304/14/37
'Bulldog' class 4-4-0s	3361, 3443 *Chaffinch*, 3444 *Cormorant*
'Dean Goods' 0-6-0	2410/8/72, 2527/37/78
'2251' class 0-6-0	2211/2/3/4, 2261/6/7/8

As 4-6-0s were not allowed on the Minehead branch, engines of through trains from Paddington to Minehead were changed at Taunton. In the 1930s this was carried out on the goods loop, but in the 1950s at the passenger station. Passenger trains on the branch were limited to a maximum of nine coaches, so any in excess of this number were removed at the same time.

When Watchet was the branch terminus it had a single road engine shed built of timber, the roof slated. In front of it was a tank, its water supply piped from Mill Pond. The shed was sited beside the main line at the east end of the passenger station, immediately east of Govier's Lane crossing. The 37 ft 8 in. diameter turntable was a little further east on the opposite side of the line. With the opening of the Minehead Railway in July 1874, both the shed and turntable were dismantled and moved to Minehead where the former stayed until closure on 3rd November, 1956. Minehead

A '43XX' class 2-6-0 leaves the turntable at Minehead *c.* 1955. The engine shed is to the right of the photograph. *M.E.J. Deane*

'4575' class 2-6-2T No. 5533 and '43XX' class 2-6-0 No. 6373 outside the engine shed at Minehead *c.* 1958. A horse box stands right, at the end of the bay platform. The turntable road is on the left. *M.E.J. Deane*

was a sub-shed to Taunton, the latter providing engines after 3rd November, 1956. On 31st December, 1947 the locomotive allocated to Minehead was '2251' class 0-6-0 No. 2213.

When Minehead passenger station was altered in 1905 to have two platform faces, the turntable was removed from a position north of the shed, to one on the south side. It was probably then that a 45 ft diameter table was installed. When 4-4-0 or 2-6-0 engines were turned, extension ramps had to be used for supporting the tender. These were not popular with footplate crews because they did not allow the engine to be well-balanced and thus could be difficult to turn.

These cast steel extensions, approximately 6 ft in length and weighing about 5 cwt. each, were hinged so that before an engine longer than the table ran on, these extension pieces could be rolled over on top of the rails at one end. The extensions were rolled over using 4 ft long bars which slotted into holes in the extensions. The pieces tapered like a wedge and their outward ends were bent into a sharp curl to form a wheel stop. The procedure was to make sure that, before going on the table, the extensions were at the Taunton end; the engine was then run over the table to the short siding beyond; the extensions were then folded down on to the rails and the locomotive reversed on to them. The engine was then turned, run off the table and the extensions folded down clear of the running rails. It was essential that the tender, and not the engine, was on the extension, otherwise the coupled wheels would become 'locked up' and the locomotive impossible to move. This happened on at least one occasion, but fortunately another engine was nearby and drew it off. 'Bulldogs' were the trickiest to turn on this table as, when on the extension, the centre pair of tender wheels was clear of the rails and therefore no use for hand-braking; as there was no handbrake on the engine, the turntable had to be swung as quickly as possible before the vacuum brake leaked off the engine. At the date of its removal in 1966, it was one of the very few extant examples with an extension ramp. The last engine to use the turntable was ex-LMS Stanier Pacific No. 46229 *Duchess of Hamilton*, which arrived hauled by 0-6-0PT No. 9647, for display at Butlin's holiday camp. Due to its length, locomotive and tender had to be turned separately. In 1975 No. 46229 left behind type '2' Bo-Bo No. 5209 for overhaul at Swindon before going to the National Railway Museum, York.

Many of the branch engines were stabled at Taunton. The first shed there was a 2-road affair built of timber. It closed in April 1896 and was replaced at a cost of £10,500 by a shed constructed of brick. The adjacent raised coaling stage was provided with a 35,000 gallon water tank above. The 28 radiating roads within the shed held a total of 26 locomotives, an incoming and an outgoing road having to be kept clear. In its early years, if not initially, the turntable was worked by electric power, but because some crews halted it by reversing the motor, (thus risking blowing a fuse), rather than using the footbrake, it was converted to hand operation around 1936. In 1932 a standard design repair shop built of corrugated asbestos was erected between the shed and No. 4 bay platform.

Miles	PASSENGER DOWN TRAINS.	ON WEEK DAYS.																SUNDAYS.		
		1	2	3	4	5	6	7	8	9	10	11	12	13	14	15		1	2	3
		Mail 1, 2	Mail 1, 2	Class 1, 2	Class 1 2	Class 1 2 3	Exp. 1, 2	Class 1, 2	Exp. 1, 2	Class 1, 2	Class 1, 2	Class 1. 2	Class 1, 2	Class 1, 2	Exp. 1, 2	Class 1, 2		Mail 1, 2	Class 1, 2	Class 1,2,3
		p.m	a.m	a.m	a.m	a.m	a.m	p.m.	a.m	a.m	p.m	p.m	p.m	p.m	p.m	p.m	..	p.m	a.m	p.m
	Paddington .. Departure	8 10	..	..	..	6 0	9 15	..	11 45	10 45	..	..	2 0	..	4 50	..	..	8 10	..	2 15
	BRISTOL	12 40	6 45	8 0	9 50	11 20	12 35	1 50	2 30	3 5	4 40	..	5 50	..	8 0	8 15	..	12 40	6 45	6 50
5½	Bourton	..	..	8 12	..	11 35	..	..	..	..	4 50	..	..	..	..	..	..	..	..	..
8	Nailsea	..	7 0	8 22	10 5	11 45	..	2 5	..	3 21	4 57	..	..	..	..	8 32	..	..	7 0	7 8
12	Yatton	..	7 10	8 33	10 15	12 0	..	2 15	..	3 30	5 7	..	6 10	..	..	8 43	..	..	7 10	7 22
16	Clevedon { Dep. for D. tr.	..	7 0	8 20	10 5	11 50	..	2 5	..	3 15	4 50	..	6 0	..	..	8 30	..	..	7 0	7 5
	Clevedon { Arrv. from do.	..	7 25	8 45	10 25	12 10	..	2 25	..	3 40	5 17	..	6 32	..	..	8 55	..	..	7 18	7 37
15½	Banwell	..	7 18	8 40	10 23	12 7	..	2 23	..	..	5 15	..	..	..	..	8 49	..	..	7 18	7 36
18½	Weston-s.-Mare Junction	1 15	7 25	8 52	10 30	12 15	..	2 30	..	3 41	5 25	..	6 21	..	8 30	8 55	..	1 15	7 25	7 45
20	Weston { Dep. for Dn. tr	1 0	7 15	..	10 20	12 0	..	2 20	..	3 30	..	..	6 10	..	8 20	..	..	1 0	7 15	7 35
	Weston { Arrv. from do.	1 35	7 30	9 0	10 40	12 25	..	2 40	..	3 50	5 40	..	6 30	..	8 40	9 10	..	1 35	7 35	7 55
27	Highbridge	..	7 40	..	10 45	12 37	..	2 45	..	4 0	..	..	6 37	..	8 45	..	..	..	7 40	8 5
	Burnham { Dep. for Dn. tr.	..	7 27	..	10 28	12 25	..	2 30	..	3 48	..	..	6 20	..	8 26	9 10	..	..	..	7 50
	Burnham { Arr. from do.	..	8 6	..	10 58	12 48	..	2 56	..	4 13	..	..	6 58	..	8 58	..	..	..	7 45	8 13
	S. C. Rail. Highbridge .... Dep.	..	8 0	9 10	11 10	12 0	..	2 50	..	4 20	5 20	..	7 0	..	..	..	..	..	8 20	8 20
12	S. C. Rail. Glastonbury	..	8 48	9 37	11 50	12 35	..	3 20	..	4 55	5 49	..	7 40	..	..	..	..	..	9 5	9 13
17½	S. C. Rail. Wells .... Arriv.	..	9 0	9 47	12 2	12 45	..	3 35	..	5 5	..	..	7 52	..	..	..	..	..	9 17	9 25
33	Bridgwater	1 40	7 55	..	11 0	12 50	1 20	..	..	4 12	..	..	6 50	..	8 55	..	..	1 40	7 55	8 28
39	Durston	..	8 5	..	11 15	1 35	..	..	..	4 24	..	..	..	..	..	..	..	..	8 5	†8 38
	Yeovil Branch. Taunton .... Depart.	..	..	..	..	..	1 45	..	..	..	..	..	7 20	..	..	..	..	..	..	..
6	Yeovil Branch. Durston	..	8 45	..	11 25	2 15	2 15	..	..	4 50	..	..	7 30	..	..	..	..	..	8 10	8 50
8½	Yeovil Branch. Athelney	..	8 50	..	11 30	2 21	2 21	..	..	4 55	..	..	7 35	..	..	..	..	..	8 15	9 0
13	Yeovil Branch. Langport	..	9 5	..	11 43	2 35	2 35	..	..	5 10	..	..	7 50	..	..	..	..	..	8 30	9 10
18	Yeovil Branch. Martock	..	9 20	..	11 58	2 50	2 50	..	..	5 25	..	..	8 5	..	..	..	..	..	8 45	9 25
25	Yeovil Branch. Yeovil ....Arriv.	..	9 35	..	12 15	3 5	3 5	..	..	5 40	..	..	8 20	..	..	..	..	..	9 0	9 40
	W. S. & W. Yeovil .... Departure	..	12 5	..	1 30	4 10	4 10	..	..	..	..	..	9 5	..	..	..	..	..	..	..
	W. S. & W. Weymouth .. Arrival	..	1 15	..	2 25	5 20	5 20	..	..	..	..	..	10 0	..	..	..	..	..	..	..
44½	Taunton	2 5	8 19	..	11 29	1 50	1 37	..	3 30	4 35	..	4 50	7 12	7 20	9 15	..	..	2 5	8 19	8 53
	W. Somset. Rail. Taunton ...... dep.	..	9 50	..	..	2 5	2 5	..	5 0	5 0	..	.. { 1, 2, 3	7 30	..	..	..	..	..	..	..
	W. Somset. Rail. Bishops Lydeard	..	10 5	..	..	2 19	2 19	..	5 14	5 14	..	..	7 44	..	..	..	..	..	..	..
	W. Somset. Rail. Crowcombe Hthfleld.	..	10 19	..	..	2 33	2 33	..	5 28	5 28	..	..	7 58	..	..	..	..	..	..	..
	W. Somset. Rail. Stogumber	..	10 26	..	..	2 40	2 40	..	5 35	5 35	..	..	8 5	..	..	..	..	..	..	..
	W. Somset. Rail. Williton	..	10 35	..	..	2 49	2 47	..	5 44	5 44	..	..	8 14	..	..	..	..	..	..	..
	W. Somset. Rail. Watchet ...... arr.	..	10 40	..	..	2 55	2 55	..	5 50	5 50	..	..	8 20	..	..	..	..	..	..	..
51¾	Wellington	2 20	8 33	..	11 43	2 8	..	..	..	..	..	5 8	..	7 40	..	..	..	2 20	8 33	9 10
60¾	Tiverton Junction	2 45	8 55	..	12 5	2 38	..	..	..	..	..	5 32	..	8 5	..	..	..	2 45	8 55	9 35
65¾	Tiverton { Dep. for D. tr.	..	8 40	..	11 45	2 20	..	..	..	..	..	5 0	..	7 45	..	..	..	..	8 40	9 10
	Tiverton { Arrv. from do	..	9 20	..	12 25	2 55	..	..	..	..	..	5 50	..	8 25	..	..	..	..	9 12	9 55
63	Collumpton	2 50	9 1	..	12 11	2 45	..	..	..	..	..	5 40	..	8 13	..	..	..	2 50	9 1	9 43
67	Hele	..	9 12	..	12 22	3 0	..	..	..	..	..	5 53	..	8 28	..	..	..	..	9 12	9 58
75½	EXETER .. Arrival about	3 20	9 35	..	12 45	3 20	2 25	..	4 15	5 30	..	6 15	8 10	8 50	10 5	..	..	3 20	9 35	10 40
	Plymouth ......Arrival	5 45	12 25	..	3 55	7 25	4 40	..	..	9 25	..	..	..	..	12 10	..	..	5 45	12 25	..
	Exeter Dep. for Crediton	4 0	10 10	..	1 10	3 50	3 50	..	..	6 5	..	..	9 55	9 55	..	..	..	4 0	[illegible]	[illegible]
	Crediton Arrival	4 16	10 30	..	1 27	4 10	4 10	..	..	6 22	..	..	10 12	10 12	[illegible]	[illegible]	[illegible]	4 16	[illegible]	[illegible]

† A Train to meet this leaves Yeovil, 7 45; Martock, 8 0; Langport, 8 15; Athelney, 8 25.

Miles	PASSENGER UP TRAINS.	ON WEEK DAYS																SUNDAYS		
		1	2	3	4	5	6	7	8	9	10	11	14	13	14	15		1	2	3
		Class 1, 2	Class 1, 2	Class 1, 2	Class 1, 2	Class 1, 2	1, 2 Exp.	Class 1 2 3	Exp. 1, 2	Mail 1, 2	Class 1, 2	Fast 1, 2	Class 1 2	Class 1, 2	Class 1, 2	Mail 1, 2		Class 1,2,3	Class 1, 2	Mail 1, 2
		a.m	a.m	a.m	a.m	a.m	a.m	a.m	a.m	p.m	p.m	p.m	p.m	p.m	p.m	p.m	..	a.m	p.m	p.m
	Plymouth .... Departure	..	..	..	..	6 50	..	9 25	10 40	12 40	..	3 15	..	..	5 20	7 10	..	6 40	12 40	7 10
	Crediton .... Departure	..	..	6 55	..	9 5	9 5	10 35	11 52	1 50	4 20	4 20	..	..	..	9 5	..	7 55	2 0	9 5
	EXETER ...... Departure	..	7 5	7 40	..	9 45	10 30	12 20	12 53	3 30	4 45	5 30	..	..	8 15	9 45	..	9 30	3 30	9 45
8¼	Hele	..	7 20	..	..	10 1	..	12 40	..	3 45	5 0	..	..	..	8 30	..	..	9 50	3 45	..
12¼	Collumpton	..	7 30	..	..	10 11	..	12 52	..	3 55	5 10	..	..	..	8 40	10 7	..	10 0	3 55	10 7
14¾	Tiverton Junction	..	7 36	..	..	10 20	..	1 15	..	4 2	5 17	..	..	..	8 47	10 12	..	10 10	4 2	10 12
19¾	Tiverton { Dep. for Up tr.	..	..	..	..	10 5	..	12 55	..	3 46	5 0	..	..	..	8 30	..	..	9 50	3 46	9 10
	Tiverton { Arriv. from do.	..	..	..	..	10 35	..	1 30	..	4 18	5 50	..	..	..	9 3	..	..	10 30	4 18	..
23¾	Wellington	..	7 56	..	..	10 36	..	1 40	..	4 18	5 40	..	..	..	9 10	10 33	..	10 30	4 18	10 33
	W. Somset. Rail. Watchet .... dep.	..	..	..	..	8 45	..	12 30	12 30	3 30	..	..	..	.. { 1, 2, 3	6 15	..	..	..	..	..
	W. Somset. Rail. Williton	..	..	..	..	8 52	..	12 36	12 36	3 36	..	..	..	..	6 21	..	..	..	..	..
	W. Somset. Rail. Stogumber	..	..	..	..	9 5	..	12 49	12 49	3 49	..	..	..	..	6 34	..	..	..	..	..
	W. Somset. Rail. Crowcombe Hthfield.	..	..	..	..	9 12	..	12 56	12 56	3 56	..	..	..	..	6 41	..	..	..	..	..
	W. Somset. Rail. Bishops Lydeard	..	..	..	..	9 22	..	1 5	1 5	4 5	..	..	..	..	6 50	..	..	..	..	..
	W. Somset. Rail. Taunton .... arr.	..	..	..	..	9 35	..	1 18	1 18	4 18	..	..	..	..	7 3	..	..	..	..	..
30¾	Taunton	..	8 15	8 26	..	11 13	11 8	1 55	1 33	4 33	6 0	6 12	..	..	9 25	10 50	..	10 45	4 33	10 50
	W. S. & W. Weymouth .. Depart.	..	..	6 10	..	9 0	..	..	..	1 0	..	3 45	..	..	..	..	..	..	..	..
	W. S. & W. Yeovil .... Arriv.	..	..	7 0	..	10 10	..	..	..	1 50	..	4 55	..	..	..	..	..	..	..	..
	Yeovil Branch. Yeovil .... Departure	..	..	7 10	..	10 20	..	12 25	12 25	3 30	..	6 10	..	..	6 10	..	..	7 5	3 40	..
7	Yeovil Branch. Martock	..	..	7 25	..	10 35	..	12 37	12 37	3 45	..	6 22	..	..	6 22	..	..	7 20	3 55	..
12	Yeovil Branch. Langport	..	..	7 37	..	10 47	..	12 49	12 49	3 58	..	6 34	..	..	6 34	..	..	7 35	4 10	..
16½	Yeovil Branch. Athelney	..	..	7 48	..	10 59	..	12 59	12 59	4 9	..	6 44	..	..	6 44	..	..	7 45	4 20	..
19	Yeovil Branch. Durston	..	..	8 0	..	11 5	..	1 7	1 7	4 15	..	6 52	..	..	6 52	..	..	7 55	4 25	..
25	Yeovil Branch. Taunton ...... Arriv.	..	..	..	..	..	..	..	1 18	..	..	7 5	..	..	7 5	..	..	..	..	..
36¾	Durston ...... Departure	..	..	8 38	..	11 23	..	2 9	..	4 45	..	..	..	..	..	..	..	10 55	†4 45	..
42¼	Bridgwater	..	..	8 50	..	11 34	..	2 26	1 52	4 59	..	6 32	..	..	9 52	11 15	..	11 10	4 59	11 15
	S. C. Rail. Wells ....Depart.	..	..	7 45	..	9 57	10 50	12 50	..	3 10	...	5 35	8 0	..	8 32	..	..	9 22	6 20	..
5¾	S. C. Rail. Glastonbury	..	..	8 15	..	10 7	11 17	1 0	..	3 20	4 30	5 50	8 12	..	9 0	..	..	9 42	6 45	..
17½	S. C. Rail. Highbridge .. Arrival	..	..	8 51	..	10 35	11 45	1 32	..	3 50	4 55	6 28	8 38	..	9 35	..	..	10 16	7 21	..
48½	Highbridge	..	..	9 5	..	11 49	..	2 44	..	5 10	..	6 45	8 40	..	10 5	..	..	11 34	5 10	..
.	Burnham { Dep. for Up tn.	..	..	8 35	..	11 25	..	2 32	..	4 55	..	6 20	8 26	..	9 10	..	..	11 20	..	..
	Burnham { Arr. from ditto	..	..	9 18	..	12 0	..	2 56	..	5 23	..	6 58	8 58	..	..	..	..	11 46	..	..
57	Weston Junction	..	..	9 23	..	12 9	..	3 7	..	5 25	..	7 0	8 55	..	..	11 40	..	11 58	5 25	11 40
58½	Weston { Dep. for Up trn.	6 55	..	9 13	9 20	12 0	..	2 57	..	5 15	6 0	6 50	..	9 25	..	11 25	..	11 48	5 15	11 25
	Weston { Arriv. from Do.	..	..	9 40	..	12 25	..	3 15	..	5 35	..	7 10	9 10	..	..	11 55	..	12 8	5 35	11 55
60	Banwell	7 7	..	..	9 35	12 17	..	3 15	..	..	6 12	..	9 2	..	..	..	..	12 8	..	..
63½	Yatton	7 15	..	..	9 45	12 29	..	3 27	..	5 40	6 22	..	9 12	9 40	10 40	..	..	12 20	5 40	..
67½	Clevedon { Dep. for Up tr.	7 0	..	..	9 35	12 15	..	3 15	..	5 30	6 0	...	8 30	..	..	..	..	12 10	5 30	..
	Clevedon { Arriv. from do.	7 25	..	..	9 56	12 40	..	3 40	..	5 50	6 32	..	..	..	..	..	..	12 30	5 50	..
67½	Nailsea	7 24	..	..	9 56	12 39	..	3 37	..	5 55	6 32	..	..	..	..	..	..	12 34	5 55	..
70	Bourton	7 29	..	..	10 3	..	..	..	..	..	6 40	..	9 22	..	..	..	..	..	..	..
75½	BRISTOL ..Arrival about	7 40	..	10 5	10 18	1 0	12 12	4 0	2 45	6 15	7 0	7 30	9 45	10 10	11 15	12 25	..	1 0	6 15	12 25
	Paddington	11 15	..	2 5	..	5 5	3 0	8 50	6 0	11 0	..	11 0	..	..	..	4 35	..	6 0	11 0	4 35

† A Train leaves Durston, 4 50; Athelney, 5 0; Langport, 5 10; Martock, 5 25.

Working timetable, April 1862.

Chapter Nine

Timetables

The service to Watchet opened with four trains each way on weekdays only, stopping at all stations, down trains taking 50 minutes and most up trains 48 minutes. Two carried third class passengers, the others having only first and second accommodation. The first timetable stated: 'This line will open a direct route to Lynton, Porlock, Minehead &c, and well regulated coaches will run from Williton in connection with the Expresses and third class trains'. In 1866 the *Defiance* coach, after the arrival of the 11.00 am train from Taunton, left Williton station for Dunster and Minehead, returning to connect with the 6.21 pm up train. The Royal Mail coach *Prince of Wales* linked Williton and Lynton taking about 4½ hours. With the opening to Minehead in July 1874 the frequency remained the same, trains taking 1 hour 20 minutes Taunton to Minehead and vice versa. By 16th September, 1882 there was discontent with the train service, the *West Somerset Free Press* of that date recording:

> A well-attended meeting was held at Williton for the purpose of discussing the deficiency in the Minehead branch train service. Sir Alexander Hood, who presided, spoke of dissatisfaction in the district owing to the reduction of trains during the last winter service. The fact was that many of the local gentry had subscribed, some to a large amount, in order to get the line constructed and now they had got it, it was of very little use to them. The late Sir Peregrine Acland and himself found £70,000 of the money which was required, but they would not have done so had they not held every hope that the line would be so worked as to be a convenience to the neighbourhood.
>
> One speaker said that a man living at Porlock wishing to have a day at Taunton, had to get up at five in the morning to catch the first train from Minehead in order to get back by a reasonable hour. If he left Minehead by the second train, he could not get home until ten at night.
>
> This meeting, it was stated, had immediate results in augmenting the train service.

In August 1887 five trains ran each way, the fastest taking 1 hour 10 minutes. The frequency was the same in April 1910, though there was an additional train including a coach slipped at Taunton from a down train from Paddington. Another extra train ran on Fridays and Saturdays non-stop from Taunton to Minehead in 52 minutes, though it would set down at intermediate stations on notice being given to the guard. Five up trains were run, one, departing from Minehead at 9.30 am on Friday and Saturdays, only making scheduled stops at Watchet and Williton, though it would call if required at other stations to take up for Bristol and beyond - 'Notice to be given to the respective Station Masters not later than 9 am'. In October 1914 the service still showed five trains each way, though some ran to or from Yeovil rather than Taunton. By July 1922 seven trains ran each way plus one on Fridays only. Down through coaches from Paddington stopped only at Williton, Watchet and Dunster. Local trains at this period consisted of a 'WW' set of 4-wheelers comprising: van third, third, composite and another van third. The 1933 summer service gave the first non-stop runs over the branch for some years, that in the down direction taking 48 minutes on Fridays and Saturdays.

MINEHEAD BRANCH.

Single Line worked by Electric Train Staff. The Crossing Stations are Norton Fitzwarren, Bishop's Lydeard, Crowcombe, Williton, Blue Anchor, and Minehead.
The Staff Stations are Norton Fitzwarren, Bishop's Lydeard, Crowcombe, Williton, Watchet, Washford, Blue Anchor, Dunster, and Minehead.
When absolutely necessary two Goods Trains, or a Passenger and a Goods Train may cross at Watchet, Washford or Dunster Stations, on the understanding that the Passenger Train is always kept on the Running Line, and that if the Passenger Train has to stop at either Station it must stop at the Platform.

Down Trains. TAUNTON TO MINEHEAD. Week Days only.

Distance from Taunton M.	C.	STATIONS.	Station No.	1 K Goods. arr.	1 K dep.	2 B Passenger. arr.	2 B dep.	3 B Yeovil Passenger. arr.	3 B dep.	4	4	5 K Goods. arr.	5 K dep.	6 B Passenger. arr.	6 B dep.	7	8 B SUS-PEN-DED.	9 A Passenger. FSO arr.	9 A dep.	10 B Weymouth Passenger. arr.	10 B dep.	11	11	12 B Passenger. arr.	12 B dep.
				A.M.	A.M.	A.M.	A.M.	A.M.	A.M.			P.M.	P.M.	P.M.	P.M.		P.M.	P.M.	P.M.	P.M.	P.M.			P.M.	P.M.
—	—	**Taunton** ...	1518	—	6 15	—	**8 2**	**9 55**	**11 17**	..	..	—	12 30	—	**1 48**	....	*3 37*	—	*4 40*	**5 20**	**5 45**	..	..	—	**7 46**
2	1	Norton Fitzwarren	1528	R C S		—	8 8	—	11 23	....	....	12 37	12 45	—	1 54	..	X CS	—	—	5 50	5 52	....	....	7 51	7 53
5	9	Bishop's Lydeard	1582	6 33	6 45	—	8 15	—	11 30	..	..	1 0	1 30	2 0	X 2 3	....	CS	V See note		5 58	6 0	..	..	—	8 0
8	78	Crowcombe ..	1583	7 0	7 7	—	8 25	11 39	X 11 42	....	....	1 45	X 2 30	—	2 13	..	CS			6 9	X 6 11	....	....	8 9	X 8 13
11	52	Stogumber	1584	7 17	7 39	—	8 31	—	11 48	..	..	2 40	2 50	—	2 19	....	CR			—	6 17	..	..	—	8 19
14	73	Williton ..	1585	7 49	8 5	8 36	X 8 39	11 53	11 55	....	....	3 0	3 40	2 24	2 26	..	CS X			6 22	6 25	....	....	8 24	8 26
16	52	Watchet	1587	8 10	X 8 53	8 43	8 45	11 59	12 1	..	..	3 45	X 5 30	2 30	2 32	....	CS			6 29	6 32	....	..	8 30	8 32
18	79	Washford ..	1588	9 1	9 16	8 51	8 53	12 7	12 9	....	....	5 38	—	—	2 39	..	CS			—	6 39	....	....	—	8 39
21	22	Blue Anchor	1589	9 23	X 9 37	—	8 58	—	12 14	..	..			2 43	2 45	...	X CS	—	—	—	6 44	..	..	—	8 44
23	9	Dunster ..	1590	9 42	10 5	9 2	9 6	12 18	12 21	....	....	..	..	2 49	2 53	..	*4 29*	—	—	6 48	6 51	....	....	8 48	8 51
24	64	**Minehead** ...	1591	10 10	—	**9 10**	—	**12 25**	—	..	..	....	....	**2 57**	—	....	*4 35*	*5 35*	—	**6 55**	—	..	..	**8 55**	—

R Calls at Norton Fitzwarren for Traffic for below Watchet only. V Call where required on Branch for Staff purposes and to set down Passengers from Bristol and beyond, and Exeter and beyond; 45 minutes allowed for non-stop, 55 minutes for stoppages.

Up Trains. MINEHEAD TO TAUNTON. Week Days only.

STATIONS.	1 B Yeovil Passenger. arr.	1 B dep.	2 B Passenger. MSO arr.	2 B dep.	3 B Yeovil Passenger. arr.	3 B dep.	4 B Yeovil Passenger. arr.	4 B dep.	5	5	6 B SUS-PENDED. arr.	6 B dep.	7 K Goods. arr.	7 K dep.	8 B Yeovil Passenger. arr.	8 B dep.	9 B Yeovil Passenger. arr.	9 B dep.	10 K Goods. arr.	10 K dep.	11	11	12 B SUS-PENDED. arr.	12 B dep.
	A.M.	A.M.	A.M.	A.M.	A.M.	A.M.	P.M.	P.M.			P.M.	P.M.	P.M.	P.M.	P.M.	P.M.	P.M.	P.M.	P.M.	P.M.			P.M.	P.M.
Minehead	—	**8 7**	—	*9 26*	—	**10 46**	—	**1 5**	....	....	Z	*3 40*	—	3 10	—	**4 10**	—	**7 28**	....	....	....	....	—	*10 45*
Dunster	—	8 12	—	*9 31*	10 50	10 52	1 9	1 11	..	..	—	*3 45*	3 15	3 33	4 14	4 16	—	7 33	..	..	..	..	W	*10 50*
Blue Anchor	—	8 17	—	*9 36*	—	10 57	1 16	1 18	....	....	—	*3 50*	3 39	3 46	—	4 21	—	7 38	....	....	....	....	—	*10 55*
Washford	—	8 23	—	*9 42*	11 2	11 4	1 23	1 25	..	..	—	*3 56*	3 54	Q 4 6	4 26	4 28	—	7 44	—	6 5	..	...	—	*11 1*
Watchet	8 28	X 8 30	*9 47*	*9 49*	11 9	11 12	1 30	1 32	....	....	—	*4 2*	4 13	Q 4 23	4 33	4 35	7 49	7 51	6 12	X 6 55	....	....	*11 6*	*11 8*
Williton	8 34	X 8 37	*9 53*	*9 55*	11 16	11 19	1 36	1 38	..	..	*4 7* X	*4 10*	4 28	X 5 10	4 39	4 41	7 55	7 57	7 0	7 5	..	..	*11 13*	*11 15*
Stogumber	—	8 45	—	*10 3*	—	11 27	—	1 46	....	....	—	*4 17*	—	Q	—	4 49	—	8 5	7 12	7 25	....	....	—	*11 23*
Crowcombe	—	8 53	—	*10 11*	11 34	X 11 40	—	1 54	..	..	—	*4 24*	5 30	X 5 40	4 56	X 4 59	8 12	X 8 15	7 35	7 45	..	..	—	*11 31*
Bishop's Lydeard	—	9 1	*10 19*	*10 23*	—	11 48	2 1	X 2 4	....	....	—	*4 34*	5 52	X 6 12	—	5 7	—	8 23	7 56	X •8 45	....	....	—	*11 39*
Norton Fitzwarren	9 7	9 10	C S		11 54	11 57	R 2 16	2 19	..	..	*4 40*	X *4 50*	6 22 S	T 6 33	5 14	5 16	8 30	8 33	C S		..	..	*11 46*	*11 48*
Taunton	**9 15**	**9 30**	*10 55*	—	**12 2**	**12 30**	**2 24**	**2 31**	....	....	*4 55*	—	6 40	—	**5 21**	**5 55**	**8 33**	**9 22**	9 15	—	....	....	*11 53*	—

Calls for Cattle, Urgent Goods or ST Goods only. Wagons to be put in position by 12.30 p.m. ex Taunton. R Five minutes allowed for Signal checks.

Working timetable, October 1914.

The timetable in force from 9th July, 1934 gave an unprecedented number of 10 stopping trains each way on weekdays and five on Sundays; also two extra down stopping trains on Saturdays and two up on Fridays and Saturdays. Through services to and from London remained at two on weekdays, with one extra down on Fridays and Saturdays and one up on Saturdays. On Saturdays the morning service was provided by a through express from Paddington to Minehead which stopped only at Taunton West Loop signal box to change engines and then ran to Minehead in 47 minutes, the journey from Paddington to Minehead taking 3 hours 27 minutes. On Fridays and Saturdays the 12.05 pm from Paddington reached Minehead in 3 hours 24 minutes running non-stop from Taunton in 45 minutes. On Fridays and Saturdays through carriages from the 3.30 pm from Paddington were run from Taunton to Minehead in 51 minutes, stopping only at Dunster, and conditionally between Stogumber and Blue Anchor, arriving at Minehead 3 hours 26 minutes after leaving Paddington. On other days, the coaches were attached to the 6.30 pm stopping train, due at 7.33 pm. The 9.00 am from Paddington via Bristol conveyed through coaches except on Saturdays, arriving at 1.13 pm.

In the up direction on Saturdays the 12.15 pm, which ran non-stop between Williton and Taunton, conveyed through coaches to Paddington, taking 3¾ hours and arriving at 4.00 pm. The 1.50 pm on Saturdays, which ran non-stop to Taunton in 45 minutes, conveyed through coaches which reached Paddington at 5.30 pm; on other days the coaches travelled via the 1.15 pm stopping train. The 11.15 am stopping train conveyed through coaches which reached Paddington via Bristol at 4.05 pm. On Sundays, through coaches for Paddington ran on the 5.25 pm train, arriving at 9.30 pm. Such a service over a single line which, with its gradients and curves was difficult to work, and on which speed was limited to 55 mph, was an achievement of which the GWR could be proud. The greatest frequency on the branch was given in the 1930s, the 1938 summer timetable offering 10 stopping trains each way on weekdays,

MINEHEAD BRANCH. Single Line, Bishop's Lydeard to Dunster, worked by Electric Token. Crossing Places are Crowcombe, Leigh Bridge, Williton, Kentsford, and Blue Anchor. Washford is a Staff Station. Intermediate Token Instrument at Watchet. When necessary a Train (not conveying passengers) may be placed in the Siding at Watchet or Washford for another train or trains to pass in the same or opposite direction.

DOWN TRAINS. WEEK DAYS.

M.P. Mileage from Padd. M.	C.	Dist. from T'nt'n. M.	C.	STATIONS.	Time Allowance for Ordinary Freight Trains, see page 2. Point-to-Point Times.	Allow for Stop.	Allow for Start.	Ruling Gradient.	K Goods. arr.	dep.	B Passenger. arr.	dep.	B Pass. dep.	B Pass. SO dep.
					Mins.	Mins.	Mins.		a.m.	a.m.	a.m.	a.m.	a.m.	a.m.
163	11	—	—	**TAUNTON**	—	—	2	—	—	**5 40**	—	**7 20**	**8 10**	9 10
165	8	1	77	Norton Fitzwarren	5	1	1	—	5	47	7	24	8 15	9 15
168	20	5	9	Bishop's Lydeard	10	1	2	93 R.	5 58S	T6 5	7 30	7 32	8X22	9 23
172	10	8	79	Crowcombe	13	1	1	80 R.	6 20S	T6 25	7 39	7 41	8 29½	9 32
174	8	10	77	Leigh Bridge	—	—	—	93 F.	—	—	—	—	—	YCS
174	64	11	53	Stogumber	7	2	1	98 F.	—	—	7 46	7 47½	8 35½	9 38
178	6	14	75	Williton	8	2	1	91 F.	6 42	6 56	7 53	X7 59	8 44	X9 55
179	64	16	53	Watchet	5	1	2	147 F.	7 2	7 7	8 2½	8 4½	8 48½	10 0
180	40	17	29	Kentsford	—	—	—	82 R.	—	—	—	—	—	CS
182	11	19	0	Washford	7	1	1	76 R.	7 16	7 30	8 9½	8 11½	8 54½	10 6½
184	34	21	23	Blue Anchor	6	1	1	66 F.	7 36	X 7 45	8 15½	8 18	8 59½	10 12
186	21	23	10	Dunster	4	1	1	80 F.	7 50	8 5	8 21½	8 25	9 6	10 19
187	71	24	60	**MINEHEAD**	4	1	—	224 F.	8 10	—	**8 28**	—	**9 9**	10 23

STATIONS.	B Passenger. SX arr.	dep.	B Passenger. SO arr.	dep.	K Goods. SX arr.	dep.	B Passenger. SX N arr.	dep.	A 9.35 a.m. Paddington Pass. SO July 8th to September 2nd, inclusive. arr.	dep.
	a.m.	a.m.	a.m.	a.m.	a.m.	a.m.	p.m.	a.m.	p.m.	p.m.
TAUNTON	—	**10 49**	—	10 52	—	11 0	—	**11 57**	12 8	‡1215
Norton Fitzwarren	10 53	10 54	10 56	10 57	11	6	12 1	12 2	12	19
Bishop's Lydeard	10 59	11 0	11 3	11 4½	11 17	●11 30	12 7X	12 8	C12	23½S
Crowcombe	11 6½	11 7½	1111½	1113½	11 45	X12 5	1214½	1215½	C12	30½S
Leigh Bridge	C	S	C	S	12 10	X12 25	C12	19S	C12	33½S
Stogumber	1112½	1113½	1118½	1119½	12 30	12 45	1220½	1221½	—	—
Williton	11 19	11 22	11 25	X1131	12 55	X1 46	12 27	12 30	C12	39S
Watchet	1125½	1126½	1134½	1135½	1 51	1 56	1233½	1234½	—	—
Kentsford	1128½	X1133	C	S	C	S	XC12	36½S	XC12	43S
Washford	1136½	1137½	1140½	1141½	2 5	2 15	1239½	1240½	C12	46S
Blue Anchor	1141½	1142½	1145½	X1147½	2 20	2 25	1244½	1245½	C12	49S
Dunster	11 46	X1149	11 51	11 54	2 30X	2 35	12 49	12 52	C12	51½S
MINEHEAD	**11 52**	—	11 57	—	2 40	—	**12 55**	—	12 55	—

DOWN TRAINS. WEEK DAYS—continued.

STATIONS.	B Passenger. SO July 8th to September 2nd. inclusive. arr.	dep.	B Passenger. SX arr.	dep.	B Passenger. SO arr.	dep.	A Passenger SO July 8th to Sept. 9th incl. arr.	dep.	B Passenger. SX arr.	dep.	A Passenger. SO July 8th to Sept. 9th. inclusive. arr.	dep.	B Passenger. SO arr.	dep.
	p.m.	p.m.	p.m.	p.m.	p.m.	p.m.	p.m.	p.m.	p.m.	p.m.	p.m.	p.m.	arr.	dep.
TAUNTON	—	12 20	—	**1 45**	—	2 5	—V	2‡50	—	**2 50**	—	3 10	—	3 17
Norton F.	12 24	12 25	1 49	1 50	2 9	2 10	2	55	2 54	2 55	3	14	3 21	3 23
Bishop's L.	1231½	1232½	1 55	1 56	2 15X	2 16	C3	0S	3 0	3 1	C3	18½XS	3 29½	3 30½
Crowcombe	1240½	1241½	2 2½	X2 4½	222½X	2 23½	3 7*	X3 10	3 7½	X3 10	C3	25S	3 38½	3 39½
Leigh Bridge	C	S	C	S	C	S	C3	13S	C	S	C3	28S	C	S
Stogumber	1246½	1247½	2 9½	2 10½	2 28½	2 29½	—	—	3 15	3 16	—	—	3 44½	3 45½
Williton	1253½X	1256½	2 16	2 19	2 35X	2 39	C3	19S	3 21½	X324½	CX3	33S	3 51	3 54
Watchet	1 0	1 1	2 22½	2 23½	2 42½	2 43½	—	—	3 28	3 29½	—	—	3 57½	4 0
Kentsford	C1	3S	XC2	25½S	245½X	2 49	C3	23S	C	S	C3	37S	C	S
Washford	1 6	1 7	2 29	2 30	2 52½	2 53½	C3	26S	3 34½	3 35½	C3	40S	4 6	4 7
Blue Anchor	1 11½	1 12½	234½X	2 39	2 57½	2 58½	C3	29S	3 39½	X340½	C3	43S	4 11½	4 13½
Dunster	1 16	1 19	2 42½	2 45	3 2	3 5	C3	31½S	3 44	3 47	C3	45½S	4 17	4 22
MINEHEAD	1 23	—	**2 48**	—	3 8	—	3 34	—	**3 50**	—	3 48	—	4 27	—

STATIONS.	B Passenger. arr.	dep.	B Passenger. Starts from Paddington at 2.15 p.m. on Sats. arr.	dep.	A Passenger. FSO arr.	dep.	B Passenger. SX arr.	dep.
	p.m.	p.m.	p.m.	p.m.	p.m.	p.m.	p.m.	p.m.
TAUNTON	—	**4 40**	—	**5 15**	—	6 8	—	**6 35**
Norton F.	4 44	Q445	5 19	5 20	6	11½	6 39	6 40
Bishop's L.	4 50	4 51½	5 25	5 26	C6	16S	6 45	6 46
Crowcombe	4 58	5 0	5 32½	5 33½	C6	22½S	6 52½	X653½
Leigh Bridge	C5	X4S	5 37½	X5 42	CX6	25½S	C6	57S
Stogumber	5 6	5 7	5 44	5 45	Z	—	6 58½	6 59½
Williton	5 12½	5 15½	5 50½	X553½	ZC6	33½S	7 5	X7 8
Watchet	5 19	5 20	5 57	5 58	Z	—	7 11½	7 12½
Kentsford	XC5	22S	C6	0S	C6	41S	C7	14½S
Washford	5 25	5 26	6 3	6 4	ZC6	44S	7 17½	7 18½
Blue Anchor	5 30	5 31	6 8	6 9	ZC6	49XS	7 22½	7 23½
Dunster	5 34½	5 37	6 12½	6 15	6 53½	6 56½	7 27	X7 30
MINEHEAD	**5 40**	—	**6 18**	—	7 0	—	**7 33**	—

N—also runs on Saturdays, September 9th, 16th and 23rd. **Q**—Not to call on Saturdays. **V**—When late, running time Taunton to Crowcombe 15½ minutes. **Y**—Not to be allowed to delay 9.30 a.m. Minehead; if necessary to be held at Leigh Bridge. **Z**—Calls, if necessary, to set down passengers from Taunton and beyond on notice being given to the guard at Taunton. ‡—West Loop Box.

Working timetable for 3rd July, 1939-24th September, 1939 - the last pre-war summer.

Minehead Branch—*continued.*

UP TRAINS. WEEK DAYS.

STATIONS.	Time Allowances for Ordinary Freight Trains, see page 2. Point-to-Point Times.	Allow for Stop.	Allow for Start.	Ruling Gradient.	B Pass.	B Passenger.		B Paddington Passenger. SO				B Passenger. SX		A Paddington Passenger. SO W		B Passenger. SX		B Passenger. SO		A Passenger. SO				A Paddington Passenger. SO July 8th to Sept. 16th inclusive.	
					dep.	arr.	dep.	arr.	dep.			arr.	dep.	arr.	dep.	arr.	dep.	arr.	dep.	arr.	dep.			arr.	dep.
	Mins.	Mins.	Mins.		a.m.	a.m.	a.m.	a.m.	a.m.			a.m.	a.m.	p.m.	p.m.	p.m.	p.m.	p.m.	p.m.	p.m.	p.m.			p.m.	p.m.
MINEHEAD	—	—	1	—	**7 35**	—	**9 30**	—	*11 0*	....	....	—	**11 15**	—	*12 15*	—	**1 20**	—	*1 20*	—	*1 50*	....	....	—	*2 20*
Dunster	4	1	1	224 R.	7 38½	9 33	9 34	*11 3½*	*11 5*	..	..	11 18	11 19	*12 18½*	*12 20*	1 23	1 24	*1 23*	*1 24*	C 1	53½S	..	..	C 2	23½C
Blue Anchor	4	1	1	80 R.	X7 43	9 37½	9 38½	*11 9*	*11 11*	..	....	11 22½	11 23½	*12 24*	*12 28*	1 27½	1 28½	*1 27½*	*1 28½*	C 1	56S	..	..	C 2	26C
Washford	6	1	1	66 R.	7 48	9 43	9 44	*11 16*	*11 17½*	..	..	11 28	11 29	*12 33*	*12 35*	1 33	1 34	*1 33*	*1 34*	C 2	0S	..	....	C 2	30C
Kentsford	—	—	—	76 F.	—	C	S	C	S	..	....	XC 11	32S	*12 38X*	*¶12 44*	C 1	37S	C 1	37S	C 2	2½S	..	..	C 2	32½S
Watchet	6	2	1	82 F.	7 53½	9 48½	9 49½	*11 22*	*11 25*	..	..	11 34	11 37	*12 46½*	*¶12 49*	1 38½	1 39½	*1 38½*	*1 39½*	—	—	..	..	—	—
Williton	5	1	2	147 R.	X8 0	9 53X	9 56	*11 29X*	*11 32*	..	....	11 41	11 44	*12 53X*	*¶12 57*	1 43	X1 47	*1 43*	*1 47*	C 2	7S	..	....	XC 2	37S
Stogumber	10	1	2	91 R.	8 7	10 2	10 3	*11 39*	*11 40*	..	..	11 51	11 52	—	—	1 53	1 54	*1 53*	*1 54*	—	—	..	..	—	—
Leigh Bridge	—	—	—	98 R.	—	C	S	C	S	....	....	C 11	54½S	C 1	6S	C 1	56S	C 1	56S	C 2	14S	..	..	C 2	44S
Crowcombe	8	1	1	93 R.	8 13½	10 8½	10 9½	*11 46½*	*11 48*	..	..	11 58½X	11 59½	C 1	9S	2 0	2X 4	*2 0*	*2 2*	*2*18*	*X2 24*	..	..	C 2	47½S
Bish'p's L'deard	9	2	1	80 F.	X8 22	10 16	10 17	*11 55*	*11 57*	..	....	12 6	X12 8	C 1	15S	2 11	2 12	*2 9*	*X2 10*	C 2	30S	..	..	C 2	52½S
Norton F.	8	1	1	93 F.	8 29	10 22	10 24	*12 3*	*12 6*	..	..	12 15	12 18	1	21	2 18	2 20	*2 16*	*2 19*	2	35	..	..	*2 57*C	E*3 3*
TAUNTON	5	1	1	—	**8 34**	**10 28**	—	*12 10*	*12 20*	..	..	**12 22**	—	*1 25*	*1 35*	**2 25**	—	*2 24*	—	*2 40*	—	..	..	3	7

UP TRAINS. WEEK DAYS—continued.

STATIONS.	B Passenger.		K Goods. SO		K Goods. SX		B Passenger.				B Passenger.		K Goods. SX		B Passenger. SX		B Passenger SO		B Passenger.		B Passenger. SO		B Passenger.		
	arr.	dep.	arr.	dep.	arr.	dep.	arr.	dep.			arr.	dep.	arr.	dep.	arr.	dep.	arr	dep.	arr.	dep.	arr.	dep.	arr.	dep.	
	p.m.	p.m.	a.m.	a.m.	a.m.	a.m.	p.m.	p.m.			p.m.	p.m.	p.m.	p.m.	p.m.	p.m.	p.m.	p.m.	p.m.	p.m.	p.m.	p.m.	p.m.	p.m.	
MINEHEAD	—	**2 30**	—	*11 15*	—	**11 40**	—	**4 25**	....	....	—	**5 0**	—	**3 10**	—	**6 40**	—	*6 52*	—	**7 27**	—	*8 40*	—	**9 15**	..
Dunster	2 33X	2 34	*11 20●*	*11 35*	**11 45X**	**12 0**	4 28	4 29	..	....	5 3	5 4½	**3 15**	**3 25**	6 43	6 44	*6 55*	*6 56*	7 30X	7 32	*8 43*	*8 44*	9 18	9 19	....
Blue Anchor	2 37½	X2 38½	*11 40X*	*11 50*	C	S	4 32½	4 33½	..	....	5 8	5 10	**3 30**	**X3 46**	6 47½‡	X6 48½	*6 59½*	*7 0½*	7 36X	7 37½	*8 47½*	*8 48½*	9 22½	X9 24	....
Washford	2 43	2 44	C	S	C	S	4 38	4 39	..	..	5 14½	5 16	**3 53**	**4 0**	6 53	6 54	*7 5*	*7 6*	7 42½	7 43½	*8 53*	*8 54*	9 29	9 30	....
Kentsford	CX 2	47S	C	S	C	S	C 4	42S	..	....	5 19	X5 24	C	S	C	S	C	S	7	46½	—	—	—	—	....
Watchet	2 48½	2 49½	*12 5●*	*X3 10*	**12 20●**	**X3 10**	4 43½	4 44½	..	....	5 26	5 27½	**4 6**	**●5 35**	6 58½	7 0	*7 10½*	*7 11½*	7 48	7 49	*8 58½*	*8 59½*	9 34½	9 35½	....
Williton	2 53	2 56	*3 17*	*X3 55*	**3 17X**	**3 45**	4 48	4 51	..	....	5 31½	5 34	**5 42**	**X●6 1**	7 3½	X7 8	*7 15*	*X7 19*	7 53	7 56	*9 3*	*X9 6*	9 39	9 42	....
Stogumber	3 2	3 3	—	—	—	—	4 57½	4 58	..	....	—	—	**6 13**	**6 30**	7 14	7 15	*7 25*	*7 26*	8 3	8 4	*9 12*	*9 13*	9 48	9 49	....
Leigh Bridge	C 3	5S	C	S	C	S	5 1X	5 7	..	....	XC 5	40½S	—	**Z**	C	S	C	S	—	—	—	—	—	—	..
Crowcombe	3 8½	X3 9½	C	S	C	S	5 11½	5 12½	..	....	5 44½	5 45½	**6 40**	**X6 55**	7 20½	7 21½	*7 31½*	*7 32½*	8 10½	8 12	*9 18½*	*9 19½*	9 55	9 56	....
Bishop's L.	3 16	X3 17	*4 25*	*4 30*	**4 15**	**4 30**	5 19	5 20	..	....	5 52½	5 53½	**7 7**	**7 13**	7 28	7 29	*7 39*	*7 40*	8 19	8 20	*9 26*	*9 27*	10 2½X	10 4	....
Norton F.	3 22	3 25	*4*	*40*	4	40	5 25	5 27	..	..	5 59½	6 2	7	23	7 35	7 38	*7 45*	*7 47*	8 27	8 30	*9 32*	*9 34*	10 9	10 11	....
TAUNTON	**3 30**	—	*4 47*	—	**4 47**	—	**5 32**	—	....	....	**6 7**	—	**7 30**	—	**7 42**	—	*7 51*	—	**8 35**	—	*9 38*	—	**10 15**	—	..

W—On September 9th, 16th and 23rd, 2 minutes less at Blue Anchor, 1 minute less at Washford crossing 11.57 a.m. Taunton at Kentsford, and 5 minutes earlier thence to Taunton. **Z**—On Fridays Leigh Bridge 6.21 X 6.26; Crowcombe arrive 6.35. ¶—When 9.35 a.m. Paddington running 10 or more minutes late, to pass Kentsford 12/38; depart Watchet 12.43 (advertised time) and arrive Williton 12.47 p.m. to cross (Williton advertised departure time 12.50 p.m.). ‡—On Fridays 2 minutes later Blue Anchor to Williton when 6.8 p.m. Taunton to time. When latter late to proceed to Kentsford to cross.

Working timetable for 3rd July, 1939-24th September, 1939,

Minehead Branch—*continued.*

DOWN TRAINS. WEEKDAYS—continued.

STATIONS.	B Passenger. SO arr.	B Passenger. SO dep.	B Passenger. arr.	B Passenger. dep.	B Passenger. FO July 7th to Sept. 8th, inclusive. arr.	B Passenger. FO July 7th to Sept. 8th, inclusive. dep.	B Passenger. SO arr.	B Passenger. SO dep.		
	p.m.	p.m.	p.m.	p.m.	p.m.	p.m.	p.m.	p.m.		
TAUNTON	—	6 47	—	**8 30**	—	9 55	—	11 10	..	..
Norton Fitzwarren	6 51	6 52	8 34	8 35	9	59	11	14	....	....
Bishop's Lydeard	6 57	6 58	8 40	8 42	10 4	X10 5	11 19	11 20	..	..
Crowcombe	7 4½	7 5½	8 48½	8 49½	1011½	10 13	11 28	X1129	....	....
Leigh Bridge	C	S	—	—	—	—	—	—	..	..
Stogumber	7 10½	7 11½	8 54½	8 55½	Z	—	11 34	11 35	....	....
Williton	7 17	X7 20	9 1	X9 5	10 23	10 26	11 41	11 44	..	..
Watchet	7 23½	7 24½	9 8½	9 10	1029½	1030½	1147½	1148½	....	....
Kentsford	C	S	—	—	—	—	—	—	..	..
Washford	7 29½	7 30½	9 15	9 16	ZC	S	11 54	1154½	....	....
Blue Anchor	7 35	X7 38	9 20	X9 24	ZC 10	39½ SX	1158½	1159½	..	..
Dunster	7 41½	7 44	9 27½	9 30	10 43	10 46	12 3	12 5	....	....
MINEHEAD	7 47	—	**9 33**	—	10 50	—	12 8	—	..	..

DOWN TRAINS. SUNDAYS.

STATIONS.	B Passenger. arr.	B Passenger. dep.	B Passenger. arr.	B Passenger. dep.	B Passenger. arr.	B Passenger. dep.	B Passenger. arr	B Passenger. dep.	B Passenger. arr.	B Passenger. dep.	B Passenger. arr,	B Passenger. dep.	
	a.m.	a.m.	a.m.	a.m.	p.m.	p.m.	p.m.	p.m.	p.m.	p.m.	p.m.	p.m.	
TAUNTON	—	**9 35**	..	**11 30**	—	**1 25**	—	**2 10**	—	**3 15**	—	**7 0**	..
Norton Fitzwarren	9 39	9 40	11 34	11 35	1 29	1 30	2 14	2 15	3 19	3 20	7 4	7 5	....
Bishop's Lydeard	9 46	9 47	11 40	11 41	1 35	1 36	2 21	2 22½	3 26	3 27½	7 11	7 12	..
Crowcombe	9 55	9 56	11 48	X1150	1 44X	1 45	2 30½	2 31½	3 35½	X3 40	7 19	7 20	....
Leigh Bridge	—	—	—	—	—	—	—	—	—	—	—	—	..
Stogumber	10 1	10 2	11 55	11 56	1 50	1 51	2 36½	2 37½	3 45	3 46	7 25½	7 26½	....
Williton	10 7½	1010½	12 1½	12 4½	1 56½	1 59½	2 43	2 46	3 51½	3 54½	7 32	7 35	..
Watchet	10 14	1015½	12 8	12 10	2 3	2 5	2 49½	2 50½	3 58	3 59	7 38½	7 39½	....
Kentsford	—	—	—	—	—	—	—	—	—	—	—	—	..
Washford	10 21	10 22	1215½	1216½	2 11	2 12	2 56	2 57	4 4½	4 5½	7 45	7 46	....
Blue Anchor	1026½	1027½	12 21	12 22	2 16½	2 17½	3 1½	X3 2½	4 10	4 11	7 50½	7 51½	..
Dunster	10 31	10 32	1225½	12 27	2 21	2 22	3 6	3 7	4 14½	4 16	7 55	7 56	....
MINEHEAD	**10 35**	—	**12 30**	—	**2 25**	—	**3 10**	—	**4 20**	—	**7 59**	—	..

UP TRAINS. WEEKDAYS—continued.

STATIONS.	B Passenger. FSO arr.	B Passenger. FSO dep.			G Engine FO July 7th to Sept. 8th, inclusive. arr.	G Engine FO July 7th to Sept. 8th, inclusive. dep.				
	p.m.	p.m.			p.m.	p.m.				
MINEHEAD	—	10 50	..	..	—	11‖20	..	..	..	..
Dunster	10 53	10 54	....	....	C	S	....	....	....	....
Blue Anchor	1057½	1058½	..	..	C	S	..	..	..	..
Washford	11 3	11 4	....	....	C	S	....	....	....	....
Kentsford	—	—	....	..	—	—	..	..	..	..
Watchet	11 8½	11 9½	..	....	—	—	....	....	....	....
Williton	11 13	11 15	....	..	C	S	..	..	..	..
Stogumber	11 21	‡1122	..	....	—	—	....	....	....	....
Leigh Bridge	—	—	....	..	—	—	..	..	..	..
Crowcombe	1127½	X1131	..	....	C	S	....	....	....	....
Bishop's Lydeard	11 38	11 39	....	..	C	S	..	..	..	..
Norton Fitzwarren	11 45	11 47	..	....	12	15	....	....	....	....
TAUNTON	11 53	—	....	..	12‖20	—	..	..	..	..

UP TRAINS. SUNDAYS.

STATIONS.	B Passenger. arr.	B Passenger. dep.	B Passenger. arr.	B Passenger. dep.	B Passenger. arr.	B Passenger. dep.	B Passenger. dep.	B Passenger. arr.	B Passenger. arr.	B Passenger. dep.	B Passenger. arr.	B Passenger. dep.	
	a.m.	a.m.	p.m.	p.m.	p.m.	p.m.	p.m.	p.m.	p.m.	p.m.	p.m.	p.m.	
MINEHEAD	—	**11 5**	..	**1 5**	—	**2 52**	—	**5 25**	—	**7 55**	—	**8 35**	..
Dunster	11 8½	11 9½	1 8	1 9	2 55½	2 57	5 28½	5 29½	7 58	7 59½	8 38½	8 39½	....
Blue Anchor	1113½	1114½	1 12½	1 13½	3 1	X3 3	5 33½	5 34½	8 3	8 5	8 43½	8 44½	..
Washford	1119½	1120½	1 18	1 19	3 8	3 9	5 39½	5 40½	8 9½	8 10½	8 49½	8 50½	....
Kentsford	—	—	—	—	—	—	—	—	—	—	—	—	..
Watchet	11 25	11 26	1 23½	1 24½	3 13½	3 15	5 45	5 46	8 15	8 16½	8 55	8 56	....
Williton	11 30	11 33	1 28	1 31	3 19	3 22	5 50	5 53	8 20	8 23	9 0	9 3	..
Stogumber	11 40	11 41	1 37	1 38	3 29	3 30	6 0	6 1	8 29	8 30	9 10	9 11	....
Leigh Bridge	—	—	—	—	—	—	—	—	—	—	—	—	..
Crowcombe	1147½X	1148½	1 43½	X1 46	336½X	3 38½	6 7½	6 8½	8 35½	8 36½	9 17½	9 18½	....
Bishop's Lydeard	1155½	1156½	1 52½	1 53½	3 45½	3 46½	6 15½	6 16½	8 43	8 44	9 25½	9 26½	..
Norton Fitzwarren	12 2½	12 5	1 58½	2 1	3 52½	3 55	6 22½	6 25	8 50	8 53	9 32½	9 35	....
TAUNTON	**12 9**	—	**2 5**	—	**3 59**	—	**6 29**	—	**8 58**	—	**9 39**	—	..

Z—Calls to set down passengers on notice being given to the guard at Taunton. ‡—To call on Saturdays only.

Working timetable for 3rd July, 1939-24th September, 1939.

plus four non-stop Saturday through trains, of which two ran non-stop from Paddington. There was only one up non-stop to Taunton and another to Paddington. Six stopping trains were provided on Sundays. The journey time of most stopping trains was one hour, while the fastest non-stop service took 40 minutes. The speed limit of 55 mph was sometimes exceeded, W.R. Webster recording on 5th April, 1940 2-6-2T No. 5522 reaching 60 mph between Bishop's Lydeard and Norton Fitzwarren with four coaches. The winter service 1938-39 gave eight stopping trains on weekdays and two on Sundays.

World War II and the immediate post-war years had seven trains each way. By 1950 the summer timetable offered 11 weekday and five Sunday trains, while the summer of 1961 showed nine on weekdays, 16 on Saturdays and six on Sundays. The last timetable, 1970-71, gave nine trains each way on weekdays, with one extra on Fridays and Saturdays, while in the summer of 1970, there was a through train from and to Paddington and on Sundays one train from Bristol.

Before dieselisation, stopping trains consisted of 'B' sets, though from early 1961 Hawksworth slip coach conversions Nos. 7374-6, with their slip gear removed, were used.

Excursion Traffic

Particularly in the early years, rail and sea excursions were run. On 1st September, 1863 a 15-coach train carrying 1,000 passengers was run from Taunton to Watchet where steamers conveyed them to Ilfracombe. Unfortunately one of the three steamers failed to arrive and so several hundred holidaymakers had to be content with a day at Watchet.

On 23rd August, 1870 a 'monster excursion' ran from Watchet to Weston-Super-Mare, the fare being one shilling return. This train carried 1,250 passengers from the Watchet branch 'including a large number of labourers, who, at the close of the harvest, were given this treat by their employers instead of a supper'. A further 1,750 joined the train at Taunton where it was divided into two. They returned from Weston-Super-Mare at 6.45 pm, some arriving at Watchet at 11.00 pm and the remainder by another train at midnight. Many carried by the latter lived on the Brendon Hills and did not arrive home until about 1.00 am.

The first excursion to Minehead was on 25th July, 1874 when, on their annual outing, over 800 employees and friends of the Bristol Waggon Works Company arrived Minehead at in a train of 15 coaches. Unfortunately the party made itself obnoxious to the inhabitants, 'Gardens were despoiled, people were insulted, goods were openly abstracted from shops without payment, fights in the streets were common, and all sorts of mischief was committed'.

On 14th July, 1905 the first half-day trip was run from London to Minehead. It left Paddington at 11.50 am and arrived at 4.57 pm. The excursionists returned by the last up train departing at 9.15 pm and arrived back at Paddington at 3.30 am. The fare was six shillings.

Each Sunday from the 6th May until 24th June, 1934 a 'Holiday Haunts Express' left Bath, Bristol and Weston-Super-Mare for Watchet, Dunster and Minehead, allowing passengers to explore the area and book apartments for a longer visit later in the season. Fares for this special train varied from five to ten shillings.

Chapter Ten

Freight Traffic and Branch Statistics

Total receipts for the branch rose from £50,206 in 1900 to £102,822 in 1923, decreasing to £94,241 in 1937. Payment to staff rose from £2,287 in 1903 to £10,566 in 1938. Tonnage carried on the branch was:

Year	*Tonnage*
1885	1,780
1903	9,192
1923	18,755
1929	25,594
1937	42,012

Unusual traffic carried over the branch in 1906 was Lynmouth's new lifeboat *Prichard Frederick Gainer* en route by rail from Poplar to Minehead. Following its arrival on station, Lynmouth's old vessel, *Louisa,* was returned by GWR to London. The *Louisa* was the boat concerned in the famous overland launch, when due to dangerous sea conditions, it was taken over Exmoor at 1,000 ft above sea level, to be launched at Porlock Bay.

Generally two goods trips were made each way daily, the average number of wagons dealt with daily on the branch in 1925 being:

Coal & mineral		*General goods*		*No. of cans*	*No. of trucks*
forwarded	*received*	*forwarded*	*received*	*of milk p.a.*	*of livestock p.a.*
1	18	31	37	7,165	1,064

Until 1st June, 1947 'Smalls' traffic arrived in station trucks, but on this date station truck working was replaced by zonal collection and delivery. Minehead still continued to receive through wagons from Bristol and Paddington, but from other centres 'Smalls' were sent to Taunton and carried onwards by trunk road motor. This system eliminated small consignments of freight traffic from stations, keeping them only for full truck loads. In 1963 Taunton became a Freight Concentration Depot and all the remaining freight facilities on the branch were withdrawn on 6th July, 1964.

In 1867 substantial catches of sprat were landed at Watchet; a 'large quantity' was sent to Bristol by rail, nearly a ton to Wellington and over three tons to Taunton. Coal arrived by sea at Watchet and was distributed onwards by rail. This traffic grew to an annual average of 17,000 tons 1934-6, then declining sharply. In 1914 Watchet dealt with a considerable trade in grain, flour, malt and timber. Watchet's peak year was 1937 when 59,303 tons of goods were forwarded and received; 15,468 parcels dispatched, and 22,428 tickets issued including 214 season tickets. The revenue of £38,332 was only just short of the total of that of all the other branch stations, not excepting Minehead. In addition to coal for merchants and the gas works, imported esparto grass and wood pulp - sheets were required for this traffic as wagons carrying these

A busy scene at the goods yard at Watchet's Eastern Pier, 2nd July, 1934.
Brunel University: Mowat/Locomotive Collection

'8750' class 0-6-0PT No. 3787 with goods train at Watchet, 24th April, 1962. *R.E. Toop*

commodities had to be sheeted and roped to prevent damage from both weather and locomotive sparks. The district commercial inspector based at Exeter was sent to Watchet to supervise the Exeter District relief gang loading the esparto traffic to rail. The bales were quite sizeable and consumed much space in open wagons. For a while, c. 1959, an experiment was carried out using high-sided 'dog's hole' coal wagons (the nickname arose due to the design of a flap-door in the lower part of the wagon side) which enabled the load to be increased by a couple of bales. Despite the wagons being swept prior to loading, complaints arose of blackened esparto grass, so the trial ended. The pulp went to Hele & Bradninch station, while the esparto grass was taken to the local paper mill and when *Flamenco* arrived at Watchet with 1,450 tons of esparto grass, 351 wagons were required to transport it. Latterly PARTO general merchandise vans, with moveable internal partitions to prevent their contents moving around and becoming damaged during shunting operations, were specially branded for use carrying paper between Watchet and Smithfield meat market. Paper had quite a high incidence of transit damage and these PARTO vans were used as a claims prevention measure. Post-World War II the 7.30 am from Taunton to Watchet consisted of up to 18 wagons, either empty, or carrying waste paper or dyes. Between six and fourteen vans of paper were despatched daily from Kentsford paper mill. Other traffic for Watchet included up to six coal wagons weekly for the town's gasworks and military supplies for Doniford Camp. The branch's only weighbridge was at Watchet and was used principally to weigh pit props from Dunster.

Watchet had a staff of seven to eight from the 1870s until 1931 when it was reduced to six. During this period salaries and wages rose from £327 to £2,055 a year. In the 1940s the station staff consisted of the station master, goods clerk, lad goods clerk, booking clerk, lad booking clerk, two male porters, female porter, shunter and the Govier's Lane crossing keeper. The station master did not have his own office and had to share accommodation. In addition to receiving merchandise for the district's shops, vehicles, guns and supplies arrived for Doniford Camp. Sugar beet was dispatched and latterly the main use of the weighbridge at Watchet was pit props from Dunster. The Dock had two steam cranes capable of loading up to 70 trucks a day. When a vessel was in port, dockers worked a 16-hour day and the rail staff did likewise, earning overtime.

Minehead's passenger traffic peaked in 1913 when 48,578 tickets were issued. Passenger revenue was lowest at Blue Anchor and Stogumber stations which had the fewest residents in the vicinity. The number of season tickets issued from the branch stations was fairly constant, averaging 300 from 1900 to 1934. In 1934 the number of seasons issued by Minehead rose from 33 to 142, reaching 369 in 1937, while the total number of season tickets for the branch in 1939 was 1,000. Around 1960, about 2,000 passengers arrived at Minehead on a peak summer Saturday.

Automatic token exchange apparatus at Blue Anchor in August 1962. *S.A. Leleux*

Chapter Eleven

Signalling and Permanent Way

The WSR and the Minehead Railway both used the B&ER's standard disc and crossbar signals. A disc and crossbar were fitted at right angles to each other on a turning post in such a way that only a disc or crossbar could be seen at any one time. A disc signalled 'all right' and the crossbar 'danger'. Each signal was operated from its base, not from a central signal box. The 'time interval' system was used on the branch until early 1868 when the electric telegraph and the block system were introduced. Interlocking of points and signals only came to the branch in 1876. In the 1890s working was by train staff and ticket, the GWR installing the electric train staff in 1895, replaced from 1926 by tokens which were lighter in weight.

One of the improvements to the branch in the 1930s was the introduction of an automatic token-exchanging apparatus enabling speed restrictions at the changeover to be raised from 15 mph to 40 mph. This apparatus was an innovation for the GWR. Supplied by the Railway Signal Company Limited, it was based on that patented by Alfred Whitaker, locomotive superintendent of the Somerset & Dorset Joint Railway and used by that line.

An iron post set beside the track had two arms normally lying parallel with the line, but capable of being swung at right angles. In this former position a pair of steel jaws, with two teeth top and bottom, faced the train, the impact forcing the token pouch carried on the engine's apparatus into the jaws where it was firmly gripped. The pouch was made of leather and had a small loop at the top. The lower arm on the post had a half cup in which rested the pouch for the section ahead and was collected by jaws on the engine which were swung out to face the lineside apparatus, before being retracted to avoid damaging anything near the track. The installation of this token changing apparatus enabled working distant signals to be installed - hitherto such signals at crossing loops on the GWR had been fixed at 'Caution'. The first engines fitted with exchangers were those of the '4575' 2-6-2T class. The apparatus was first used on 6th July, 1934, only by non-stop trains and taken out of use at the end of the summer timetable, being returned to use on 3rd July, 1935. At first not all signal boxes were equipped with ground standards and this entailed crews having to remove a key token from one type of pouch and enclose it in another, five times during a single trip. A pouch for automatic collection had a small loop, whereas one for manual exchange had a large loop. By 1st May, 1938 the exchanging apparatus was installed at all signal boxes, except for Minehead.

The first track was 68 lb./yd bridge rail laid to broad gauge on Memel timbers measuring 10 in. by 7 in. and kept to gauge by bolts through the longitudinals fixing them to the transoms. When the gauge was narrowed, these were replaced by tie bolts. The bridge rail was still in use on the through lines at Crowcombe as late as 1923 and only the need for running heavier engines over the branch necessitated its replacement. The *Great Western Magazine* for December 1923 reported:

Private and not for Publication. Notice No. 166.

GREAT WESTERN RAILWAY

(For the use of the Company's Servants only)

EXETER DIVISION

MINEHEAD BRANCH

Introduction of Automatic Token Exchange Apparatus.

FRIDAY, JULY 6th, 1934

On the above date the Signal Engineer will bring into use Automatic Token Exchange Apparatus at the following places :

Station or Signal Box	Up or Down	Position
Crowcombe	Both	Down Side of Line—111 yards from Signal Box. Taunton End of Station. Up Side of Line—111 yards from Signal Box. Taunton end of Station.
Leigh Bridge	Both	Down Side of Line—30 yards Taunton end of Signal Box. Up Side of Line—10 yards Taunton end of Signal Box.
Kentsford	Both	Down Side of Line—32 yards Taunton end of Signal Box. Up Side of Line—6 yards Taunton end of Signal Box.
Blue Anchor	Both	Down Side of Line—56 yards from Signal Box, Minehead end of Station. Up Side of Line—56 yards from Signal Box, Minehead end of Station.
*Dunster	Both	Down Side of Line—40 yards from Signal Box, Minehead end of Station. Up Side of Line—Opposite Signal Box, Minehead end of Station.

*—Setting Down for Down Trains. Picking up for Up Trains.

The apparatus is provided on the following engines of the 2-6-2-T (45XX) type :

4581, 5501, 5502, 5503, 5521, 5537, 5542, 5543, 5551, 5571

and consists of a combined picking up and setting down pillar (except at Dunster, see note above) placed on the left-hand side of each Loop and an exchanging apparatus on the left-hand side of the engine.

SPECIAL INSTRUCTIONS FOR GUIDANCE OF SIGNALMEN.

When "Line Clear" has been obtained and a token is withdrawn, the Signalman must immediately place the token in the pillar and set the arm at right angles to the track ready for the exchange to be made. The Distant Signal must not be lowered until the token has been placed in the pillar.

After the train has passed, the arm will swing and become self-locked parallel with the track in order to effect clearance.

The token collected by the pillar after the passage of the train must be taken by the Signalman and dealt with in accordance with Standard Instructions.

When Boxes provided with switching apparatus are closed the arms of the Exchange Apparatus must be secured n the normal position by padlock.

Leaflet giving detail of introduction of the automatic token exchange apparatus, 6th July, 1934.

SPECIAL INSTRUCTIONS FOR GUIDANCE OF ENGINEMEN.

The equipment on the engine consists of an exchanger (i.e., a receiving jaw and delivering clip) fixed on the end of a slide which works through a guide on the bunker. The slide is operated by means of a handle which, by being raised or lowered, serves to unlock or lock the gear in either the "In" or "Out" positions.

The token when received must be kept in its usual position and must not be placed in the clip by the Fireman until the Distant Signal has been passed. The slide must not be pushed out until the engine is near the pillar, the exact time depending upon the speed of the train, but it must be done in sufficient time to ensure the exchanger being in the proper position and the slide locked when passing the exchange pillar.

The Fireman will be responsible for satisfying himself that the exchange has been made.

The handle must on no account be touched during the exchange otherwise there is risk of the bar being drawn back too soon and the token being missed.

Immediately the exchange has been made the token must be taken from the exchanger on the engine, and the Driver must satisfy himself he has the correct token for the section.

BEFORE TAKING THE POUCH FROM THE EXCHANGE APPARATUS ON THE ENGINE THE FIREMAN MUST LOOK AHEAD AND SATISFY HIMSELF THAT HE IS CLEAR OF SIGNAL POSTS, ETC., AND THAT IT IS SAFE FOR HIM TO LEAN FROM THE CAB FOR THIS PURPOSE.

IT IS IMPORTANT THAT AS SOON AS THE EXCHANGE HAS BEEN MADE THE SLIDE MUST BE DRAWN BACK INTO ITS NORMAL POSITION AND LOCKED TO AVOID FOULING THE PLATFORMS.

THE SPEED OF TRAINS MUST NOT EXCEED 40 M.P.H. WHEN EXCHANGING.

GENERAL INSTRUCTIONS.

Passenger Trains will be worked by engines fitted with this apparatus and **MUST BE RUN WITH CHIMNEY LEADING.** If, however, it is necessary for a Passenger Train to be worked by an engine not provided with the apparatus, or running with bunker leading, an advice must be sent to the Signal Boxes concerned of the fact, and the token must be exchanged by hand in accordance with the Standard Regulations. In such a case the Distant Signal must be kept at "Caution".

Engines of Goods and Ballast Trains will not be fitted and the tokens must be exchanged by hand in accordance with Standard Instructions.

The Automatic Exchange Apparatus has not been installed at:

Norton Fitzwarren
Bishops Lydeard
Williton
Washford

DETAILS OF EXCHANGE APPARATUS ON BRANCH

DOWN TRAINS

NOTE—Engines starting from Taunton must be equipped with a spare ring to enable transfer of the Token as shewn below.

Station or Signal Box	Method of Exchange
Norton Fitzwarren	Standard
Bishops Lydeard	Standard
Change Token from Ring to Automatic Pouch	
Crowcombe	Automatic
Leigh Bridge	Automatic
Change Token from Automatic Pouch to Ring	
Williton	Standard
Change Token from Ring to Automatic Pouch	
Kentsford	Automatic
Change Token from Automatic Pouch to Ring	
Washford	Standard
Change Token from Ring to Automatic Pouch	
Blue Anchor	Automatic
Dunster	Automatic

UP TRAINS

NOTE—Engines starting from Minehead must be equipped with a spare ring to enable transfer of the Token as shewn below.

Station or Signal Box	Method of Exchange
Dunster	Automatic
Blue Anchor	Automatic
Change Token from Automatic Pouch to Ring	
Washford	Standard
Change Token from Ring to Automatic Pouch	
Kentsford	Automatic
Change Token from Automatic Pouch to Ring	
Williton	Standard
Change Token from Ring to Automatic Pouch	
Leigh Bridge	Automatic
Crowcombe	Automatic
Change Token from Automatic Pouch to Ring	
Bishops Lydeard	Standard
Norton Fitzwarren	Standard

SPEED OF TRAINS.

The following amended speeds will operate on and from the same date:

		m.p.h.
Crowcombe	Trains entering or leaving Up Station Loop ..	40
Blue Anchor	Trains entering or leaving Down Station Loop ..	40
Dunster	Trains from double to single line	40

ALL CONCERNED TO BE ADVISED AND RECEIPT ACKNOWLEDGED BELOW.

R. W. HIGGINS,
Divisional Superintendent

A. W. H. CHRISTISON,
Locomotive Superintendent.

4th July, 1934. 582—250.

FORM OF PILOTMAN'S TICKET.

(Ticket referred to in Regulation 25 of the Regulations for Train Signalling on Single Lines by Electric Token Block System).

ELECTRIC TOKEN BLOCK SYSTEM.

PILOTMAN'S TICKET.

To be used when it is necessary to work the traffic of a single line by Pilotman during a failure of the Token apparatus, or in the case of a Token being damaged or lost.

To the Driver of..train from.. to.. ....

You are authorised to proceed from..to.., Pilotman following.

Signature of Pilotman..

Date......................................

This ticket must be given up by the Driver to the person in charge of the Token working at the place to which he is authorised to proceed, immediately on arrival.

NOTE.—Pilotman's Tickets are not used on the Great Western Railway.

ELECTRIC TRAIN TOKEN EXCHANGING APPARATUS.

1. In this Apparatus the Token is fixed in a carrier to which is attached a hoop.
2. The post on which the Signalman places the Token, and from which the Fireman takes it before he enters the Token Section, is called the " Picking up " post.

The post on which the Fireman hangs the Token, after passing through the Section, and from which the Signalman afterwards fetches it, is called the " Setting down " post.

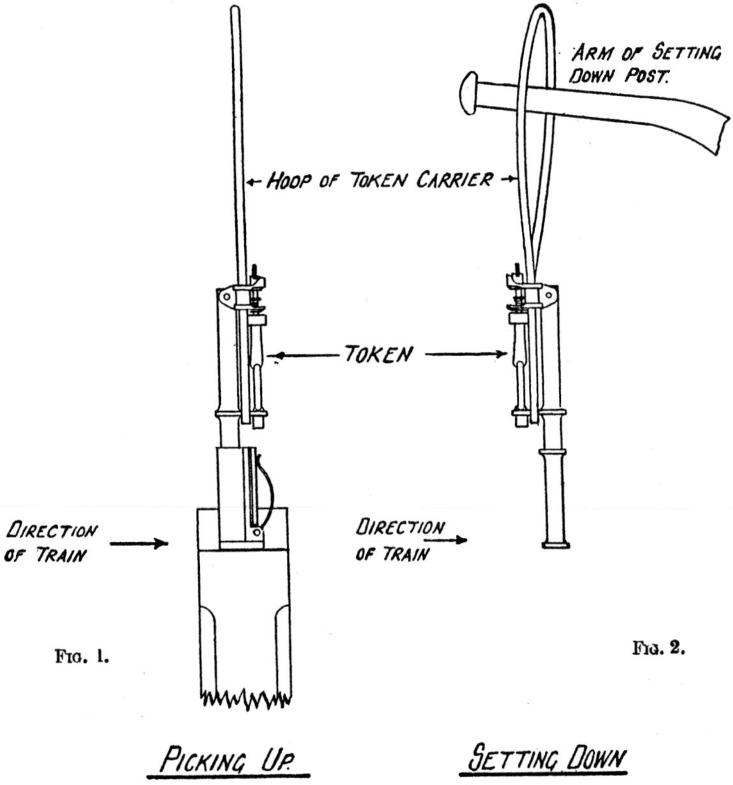

Electric token exchanging apparatus. From GWR Rule Book, 1936.

> A relic of the past is shortly to be removed from Crowcombe station, on the Minehead branch, this being a length of the bridge rail track which is one of the very few remaining portions of this track which survives in the running lines.
>
> It is only the need for the running of heavier engines on the branch which has even now rendered necessary the relaying of this portion of the line, for the road, apart from the timbers, is still good for several years for the small engines which at present work the branch.

The Minehead Railway used interlocking points and signals patented by Mr Easterbrook of the Bridgwater Engineering Company.

The main line from Taunton to Exeter was opened for mixed gauge traffic from 1st March, 1876 and the WSR Directors pressed the GWR to convert their branch to standard gauge. No immediate steps were taken, but in August 1878 James Grierson, the GWR's General Manager, recommended that the branch be converted as soon as possible to save the transfer of goods at Taunton, and also relieve the shortage of broad gauge rolling stock which was becoming acute as the company did not wish to replace worn-out vehicles in view of the eventual total abolition of the broad gauge.

The conversion was carried out over the weekend of 28th-30th October, 1882 causing little interference as no trains were run on Sundays. After the ordinary train service ended on Saturday, a special was run at about 9.00 pm to clear all broad gauge stock. Seven gangs, with about 70 men in each, attacked the 22¾ miles, each gang being responsible for about 3 miles. Work started at daybreak on Sunday and proceeded with such vigour that soon after midday a standard gauge special carrying the Divisional Engineer, Mr Hammett, and Traffic Superintendent, Mr Campfield, was able to get through to Minehead. Packing continued until 5.00 pm when the men retired, sleeping in the company's goods sheds prepared for the occasion. Work resumed on Monday morning and by 9.00 am was almost complete. Only one public passenger train ran each way, but others were run for conveying the workmen home. On Sunday the 29th, a supper had been given to about 70 of the permanent way men in the waiting room at Minehead station, paid for by a lady and two gentlemen of the town. Normal service resumed on Tuesday. The conversion cost £9,000.

Because of the gradients quite a few spring catch points were installed on the branch to guard against runaways. They were at:

Norton Fitzwarren	Either side of the down advanced starting signal
Bishop's Lydeard	Beyond the down starting signal
Crowcombe	On the down loop beyond the home signal
Leigh Bridge	On the up loop beyond the home signal and starting signal
Williton	Up loop beyond the starting signal
Kentsford	Down loop beyond the home signal and starting signal
Blue Anchor	Up loop beyond the starting signal

Williton signal box interior, 18th September, 1959. *D.J. Powell*

The signalman is seen operating the level crossing gates at Blue Anchor in this view of the signal box interior on 20th August, 1962. *S.A. Leleux*

The crossing loops varied in length:

Station	*No. of wagons in addition to engine and brake van*
Crowcombe	28
Leigh Bridge	29
Williton	31
Watchet (goods loop)	25
Kentsford	29
Washford (goods only)	11
Blue Anchor	32

From 7th November, 1932 the branch changed to the Motor Trolley System of Maintenance with gangs stationed at Bishop's Lydeard, Williton, Washford and Dunster, though by 1947 the branch had just one gang centred on Williton. The trolley could be placed upon the line after a Ganger's Occupation Key had been obtained (with the signalman's co-operation) from an instrument situated in special huts at approximately half-mile intervals. The withdrawal of an Occupation Key locked the normal token for the relevant section in its instrument, thus avoiding any possibility of a train entering the section until the trolley was removed from the line and the Occupation Key replaced in an instrument.

The signalman at Blue Anchor returns the token to the token instrument. *S.A. Leleux*

Chapter Twelve

Accidents

Few accidents were recorded about workmen constructing the line. One occurred on 14th March, 1862 when a wagon overturned at a bridge between Bishop's Lydeard and Combe Florey, its load of ballast falling on four men and severely injuring them.

On 16th May, 1870 Porter Goodman at Bishop's Lydeard had moved trucks from the main line to a siding and unfortunately omitted to re-set the points. There was no interlocking to prevent the signal being cleared and when the 11.00 am Watchet to Taunton arrived, it ran into the siding, colliding with the wagons. One wagon was smashed to pieces and a buffer was knocked from the front of the engine. Only one passenger was cut.

A similar accident happened at Watchet on 23rd August that same year. The engine of the 9.15 am had been turned and coupled to its train, but unfortunately the points were not moved so when the guard gave the 'right away', engine and train ran down the turntable road and before it could be halted, ran into the embankment at the other end, knocking the buffers from the engine. Two or three passengers were cut and bruised. Remarkably the train left only six minutes late. The pointsman was suspended.

Yet another accident occurred on 11th August, 1873 when the points being incorrectly set, the 3.35 pm Watchet to Taunton entered a siding at Williton smashing a wagon and slightly damaging the engine.

The Great Storm of 1881 closed the branch for several days as drifts in some cuttings were 30 feet deep. Ten years later in the Great Blizzard on Tuesday 10th March, 1891 the first down mail and passenger train reached Watchet, but could go no further as the line was blocked. As snow continued to fall, it was useless to start clearing it. The first up train reached Dunster, but was blocked beyond by snow six to eight feet deep for over half a mile, so it returned to Minehead. Early on Wednesday men set to work, the line being cleared from Minehead to Crowcombe, and in the afternoon an engine ran from Minehead to Watchet, returning with the down mails brought the previous day. Cuttings from Crowcombe to Bishop's Lydeard were cleared early on Thursday morning enabling the branch to be opened at 10.30 am.

Appendix One

Running Log, 31st July, 1953

Locomotive '2251' class 0-6-0 No. 2211
Four non-corridor coaches plus one corridor coach
Average speed: 31.9 mph

Distance	*Station*	*Scheduled arrival hr.min. sec.*	*Actual arrival hr.min. sec.*	*Scheduled departure hr.min. sec.*	*Actual departure hr.min. sec.*
-	Blue Anchor	- - -	- - -	11 00	11 2 53
2¼	Washford	- - -	11 6 33	11 05	11 7 30
1½	Kentsford	- - -	11 11 54		11 15 30
¾	Watchet	- - -	11 16 30	11 12	11 19 40
1¾	Williton	- - -	11 23 05	11 19	11 29 50
3¼	Stogumber	- - -	11 33 25	11 26	11 34 20
2¾	Crowcombe	- - -	11 40 23	11 33	11 41 00
4	Bishop's Lydeard	- - -	11 45 05	11 42	11 45 50
3	Norton Fitzwarren	- - -	11 54 15	11 48	11 55 35
2	Taunton	11 55	12 00 50		

Locomotive: '4575' class 2-6-2T No. 5501
Six corridor coaches
Average speed: 26 mph

Distance	*Station*	*Actual arrival hr.min. sec.*	*Scheduled departure hr.min. sec.*	*Actual departure hr.min. sec.*
-	Taunton	- - -	5 05	5 8 15
2	Norton Fitzwarren	5 13 55	5 09	5 15 16
3	Bishop's Lydeard	5 22 25	5 16	5 23 02
4	Crowcombe	5 32 20	5 24	5 32 28
2¾	Stogumber	5 38 47	5 30	5 39 45
3¼	Williton	5 45 00	5 39	5 46 38
1¾	Watchet	5 50 30	5 44	5 52 15
2¼	Washford	5 59 35	5 51	6 00 12
2¼	Blue Anchor	6 4 30	5 56	- - -

Appendix Two

Minehead Branch Locomotives from the Taunton Shedman's List and Job Allocations, 1962

2.00 pm to 10.00 pm Saturday 4th August, 1962

Time	*Working*	*Locomotive*
3.00 pm	Minehead passenger	'51XX' class 2-6-2T No. 4174
3.37 pm	Minehead passenger	'51XX' class 2-6-2T No. 4128
4.35 pm	Minehead passenger	'51XX' class 2-6-2T No. 4143
6.00 pm	Minehead passenger	BR Standard class '3MT' 2-6-2T No. 82044
7.30 pm	Minehead passenger	BR Standard class '3MT' 2-6-2T No. 82030
9.15 pm	Minehead passenger	'51XX' class 2-6-2T No. 4103

Sunday 5th August, 1962

Time	*Working*	*Locomotive*
8.50 am	Minehead passenger	'51XX' class 2-6-2T No. 4143
11.50 am	Minehead passenger	'51XX' class 2-6-2T No. 4128
2.43 pm	Minehead passenger	'61XX' class 2-6-2T No. 6146

Appendix Three

Train Staffs used on the West Somerset Railway

Between	*Colour*	*Shape*
Minehead-Blue Anchor	Blue	Tablet
Blue Anchor-Williton	Green	Square
Williton-Bishop's Lydeard	Brown	Round
Bishop's Lydeard-Norton Fitzwarren	Yellow	Triangular
Williton-Crowcombe	Red	Octagonal
Crowcombe-Bishop's Lydeard	Blue	Square

Appendix Four

A Volunteer Fireman on the West Somerset Railway
by Terry Morgan

As I am rather a new fireman on the present West Somerset Railway my experiences are naturally rather limited, especially when compared with long serving footplate crews, particularly ex-British Rail men, such as Don Haynes (Bristol, St Phillip's Marsh) and Dave Bosely (Taunton), the latter actually working on the branch at the end of steam on BR.

However, as an incentive to those who have a yearning to become a footplatemen and are prepared for the oven-like conditions of a small Prairie tank on a really hot summer's day, or the driving rain and cold wind when travelling tender first on the Collett, or any other tender engine in inclement weather, plus the 'joys' of disposal, then I would certainly recommend it.

The West Somerset Railway is very welcoming, and my own experience is of being readily accepted by a great bunch of people. A prerequisite for the privilege of footplate work is an input into locomotive restoration or similar necessary tasks. Locomotive work is at present carried out at Minehead by a mix of company employees and a steady number of volunteers, who over the years have acquired the unofficial title of 'The Iffy Rivet Company'. I came in at the end of a major overhaul to the Collett 0-6-0 No. 3205 and have witnessed the rebirth of GWR 2-6-2T No. 4160 from a heap of rusting parts into the gleaming machine she now is.

In early 1990 I had reached a certain age when I thought 'If I don't do it now, then I never will', I also had a real desire to steam into Watchet on the footplate of an engine, and perhaps see it as my great grandfather Fred had all those years ago on a B&ER Pearson 4-4-0 saddle tank.

So in the spring of that year I became an active volunteer. Aged 49, I wasn't quite the oldest trainee, a good friend Alan Mayhew, whose beard in the intervening years has grown into generous Victorian proportions, is a little older. In those first days (we have since both now admitted to one another) we wondered, 'Were we perhaps past it?' The first thing I noticed, after virtually 10 years of office work, was how unfit I was. I am now much improved on that score, and can fire up the bank from Williton to Crowcombe with barely a gasp of breath, also experience teaches you how to make the job less hard work (sometimes).

I passed my firing exam in 1992. The tests were carried out by a British Rail Inspector, and a full medical by the company doctor was required. Over the past three years, I have been fortunate to have ridden on a variety of engines. Excluding the company's stock, these include No. 4160's sister No. 6106, GWR large freight 2-8-0 No. 3822, which was to be a favourite. I admit to a GWR bias. A highlight was on a beautiful summer morning in July 1992 (the day before my birthday). I was rostered to start at Bishop's Lydeard and to my surprise, what stood on the loco' pit, her copper and brass reflecting the early sunlight, but *City of Truro*. I fired her part of the way including up the bank from Watchet to Washford. I was second man to the passed fireman at that time and naturally everybody 'wanted a go'. To actually watch those flying cranks from the footplate after previously seeing them only from the lineside as a static exhibit at Swindon, was something I shall never forget, it was a dream come true.

The 1993 season brought a magnificent black monster, LMS '8F' class 2-8-0 No. 48773 on which I had a number of turns. I found her a free steaming and powerful machine.

The route of the West Somerset Railway traverses some wonderful contrasting scenery, from the wooded slopes of the Quantock Hills to the sweep of Blue Anchor Bay. Its topography of rising and falling gradients and reverse curves make it a demanding line for the footplate crews. A wary eye is required on the gauge glass, plus the skill of

Fireman John Farley on No. 3440 *City of Truro* at Bishop's Lydeard, 26th July, 1992.

T. Morgan

maintaining a good fire for the banks, whilst not having too much when descending, is an acquired art. (The '8F' blowing off across Woolston Moor was really deafening.) The peak summer timetable, with an engine change at Williton, can involve crews in a round trip of over 60 miles.

With the new facilities at Bishop's Lydeard, this is now a regular signing on point, and rosters are usually arranged, where possible, to suit the locality of the crew. Set amongst the fields, it is for me an idyllic spot for an early turn, even though that means rising at 5 am to sign on before 7 am. There is nowhere more pleasant to have a leisurely 'light up', and prepare an engine: especially on a morning when the fresh dawn warms through to promise a glorious day, and with the reward of a good brew up, as you wait for 'her to come round', it is bliss.

The present West Somerset Railway, after early setbacks, has gone from strength to strength, and I am particularly pleased when I notice amongst the summer tourists, a passenger alight, usually at Watchet, with obvious shopping bags. It makes it doubly satisfying to know that the railway is still fulfilling, perhaps in a small way at the moment, the purpose for which it was built 130 years ago, that of serving the local community.

Terry Morgan firing *City of Truro*, 26th July, 1992. *Terry Morgan*

Prairie tank No. 5572 is seen with a goods train at Blue Anchor on 11th September, 1987.
Tom Heavyside

S&DJR '7F' class 2-8-0 No. 53808 receives attention at Minehead with GWR 0-6-0PT No. 6412 to the right on 10th April, 1988.
Tom Heavyside

Appendix Five

Current Stock List of WSR Locomotives

Steam Locomotives	*January 1998 Condition*
Class '7F' 2-8-0 No. 53808 (LMS No. 13808, S&DJR No. 88)	Awaiting major overhaul
'28XX' class 2-8-0 No. 3850	Under restoration
'Manor' class 4-6-0 No. 7820 *Dinmore Manor*	Serviceable
'Manor' class 4-6-0 No. 7828 *Odney Manor*	Serviceable
'Hall' class 4-6-0 No. 4920 *Dumbleton Hall*	On loan. Serviceable
'2251' class 0-6-0 No. 3205*	Serviceable
'5101' class 2-6-2T No. 4160	Serviceable
'45XX' class 2-6-2T No. 4561	Serviceable
'64XX' class 0-6-0PT No. 6412	Under major overhaul
Peckett 0-4-0ST ex-Kilmersdon Colliery	Serviceable
Hawthorn, Leslie 0-6-0ST No. 3437 *Isabel*	Under restoration
'West Country' class 4-6-2 No. 34046 *Braunton*	Under restoration
'Battle of Britain' class 4-6-2 No. 34053 *Sir Keith Park*	Under restoration

Diesel Locomotives	
Class '52' No. D1010 *Western Campaigner* (This locomotive has also carried the No. D1035 and nameplate *Western Yeoman*)	Serviceable
Class '35' 'Hymek' Nos. D7017, D7018	Serviceable
Class '14' 0-6-0 diesel-hydraulic Nos. D9526, D9551	Serviceable
Class '03' diesel-mechanical Nos. D2119, D2133	Serviceable
Class '04' diesel-mechanical Nos. D2205, D2271	Serviceable
Class '50' diesel-electric No. 50 017 *Royal Oak*, No. 50 149 *Defiance*	Serviceable
Class '25' diesel-electric No. 7523	Serviceable
Class '33' diesel-electric No. 33 048	Serviceable
Brush-Bagnall 0-4-0 diesel-hydraulic No. 501 (master) No. 512 (slave)	Serviceable
0-4-0 Ruston-Hornsby diesel-mechanical No. 24 (S&D Trust, Washford)	Serviceable
0-4-0 Barclay diesel-hydraulic Nos. 4, 8 (ex-Royal Ordnance Factory, Puriton)	Serviceable

Diesel Multiple Units	
Class '107' Nos. 50413, 56169	Serviceable
Class '115' Nos. 51663, 51852, 51859, 51880, 51887, 59678	Serviceable
Class '117' Nos. 59493, 59506, 59510, 59514,† 59515	Serviceable

* No. 3205 had worked on the Somerset & Dorset line during the 1960s, then on the preserved Severn Valley Railway before being transferred to the WSR in March 1987.

† Not serviceable.

Class '04' 0-6-0 diesel shunter No. D2271 shunts wagons at Minehead on 31st August, 1991.
P.G. Barnes

Class '52' 'Western' No. D1035 *Western Yeoman* runs round its train at Minehead on 31st August, 1991.
P.G. Barnes

Locomotives visiting the WSR

Visiting engines were required to operate the service as the WSR's own stud was relatively limited. Visiting engines also attracted new passengers to the line as people make a return visit to see a new sight. The first 'foreign' locomotive was '4575' class 2-6-2T No. 5572 which arrived from Didcot in 1987. Other visitors have included:

4-4-0 No. 3440 *City of Truro*
'28XX' class 2-8-0 No. 3822
'King' class 4-6-0 No. 6024 *King Edward I*
'Castle' class 4-6-0 No. 7029 *Clun Castle*
'Manor' class 4-6-0 No. 7802 *Bradley Manor*
'West Country' class 4-6-2 No. 34027 *Taw Valley*
'West Country' class 4-6-2 No. 34039 *Boscastle*
'West Country' class 4-6-2 No. 34105 *Swanage*
Ex-LMS class '4F' 0-6-0 No. 44422
'8F' class 2-8-0 No. 48773
BR Standard class '7P' 4-6-2 No. 70000 *Britannia*
BR Standard class '8P' 4-6-2 No. 71000 *Duke of Gloucester*
BR Standard class '9F' 2-10-0 No. 92220 *Evening Star*

Class '8F' 2-8-0 No. 48773, on loan from the Severn Valley Railway, leaves Williton with the 3.45 pm Minehead to Bishop's Lydeard train on 13th August, 1993. *Author*

Bibliography and Acknowledgements

Books

Bradshaw's Railway Guides

Closed Stations & Goods Depots, C.R. Clinker, Avon Anglia, 1988

The West Somerset Railway, C.R. Clinker, The Exmoor Press, 1980

Track Layout Diagrams of the GWR & BR/WR, Section 15, R.A. Cooke, 1986

A Guide to Stations & Buildings, S. Edge, P. Barnfield and E. Cubitt, WSR, 1990

The Canals of South West England, C. Hadfield, David & Charles, 1967

An Historical Survey of Great Western Locomotive Sheds 1947, E. Lyons, Oxford Publishing Co., 1972

An Historical Survey of Great Western Locomotive Sheds 1837-1947, E. Lyons & E. Mountford, Oxford Publishing Co., 1979

History of the Great Western Railway, E.T. Macdermot revised C.R. Clinker, Ian Allan, 1964

The Taunton to Minehead Railway, Minehead & District Round Table, undated.

Minehead Railway Minute Books

Branch Line to Minehead, V. Mitchell & K. Smith, Middleton Press, 1990

Locomotives of the Great Western Railway, Railway Correspondence & Travel Society, 1951-1974

The West Somerset Mineral Railway, R. Sellick, David & Charles, 1970

West Somerset Railway Stock Book, K. Smith, WSR, 1990

A Regional History of the Railways of Great Britain Vol. 1: The West Country, D. St J. Thomas, David & Charles, 1981

West Somerset Railway Minute Books

Newspapers and magazines

British Railway Journal

Railway Magazine

Taunton Courier

West Somerset Free Press

Grateful acknowledgements for assistance is due to D. Bromwich, A. Bowditch, J. Gardner, R.B. Ireland, R. Tiller and D.R. Steggles.

Special thanks must go to T. Morgan who checked the manuscript.